Inscribed
with best
wishes —

Emmett Parry

Dec. 24, 1934

BETSY ROSS
Quaker Rebel

By the Following Day She had Completed the Flag

BETSY ROSS
Quaker Rebel

BEING
THE TRUE STORY OF THE
ROMANTIC LIFE OF THE
MAKER OF THE FIRST
AMERICAN FLAG

BY

EDWIN SATTERTHWAITE PARRY
Lineal Descendant of Betsy Ross

ILLUSTRATIONS BY
J. L. G. FERRIS
AND
EDWIN JOHN PRITTIE

THE JOHN C. WINSTON COMPANY
CHICAGO   PHILADELPHIA   TORONTO

TO MY MOTHER

**A GREAT-GRANDDAUGHTER OF
THE LADY WHO IS THE CEN-
TRAL FIGURE IN THESE PAGES**

Contents

Contents

Illustrations

(ix)

Author's Note

With the exception of the Bank Meeting House, the Indian
Queen Tavern, and the Crooked Billet Tavern, all of the old
Philadelphia buildings illustrated in this book are still standing as
they were in the days of Betsy Ross. The surroundings have
changed in the forward march of the city, but the visitor finds the
historic buildings just as pictured in this narrative.

Introduction

That circumstances so dramatic as those which made up the entire life of a person as much talked about as Betsy Ross should thus far have remained in obscurity, has been a cause of wonderment to the writer of this book.

Apparently the one colorful episode that has made her name so famed in song and story was striking enough to sidetrack further delving. But the unpublished events of her career, aside from the flag incident, offer such a stirring picture of Revolutionary times that they undoubtedly belong to the nation which has such a sentimental regard for Betsy Ross, rather than to the privacy of family records; hence the decision to bring them forth and present them in a form where all may read.

Of the authenticity of the making of the first American flag, sometimes questioned, there is no real doubt through the nation at large. Betsy's high character, the truth-telling reputation of her Quaker family, and the statements of her daughters and grandchildren (some in affidavit form) to whom she often related the circumstances of the Washington interview, support the belief which has now become a historic fact to millions of Americans.

The archives of Pennsylvania clearly establish that Elizabeth Ross made flags early in the Revolution. In May, 1777, they record the payment of a bill for her handiwork some time before Congress officially endorsed the Stars and Stripes. This authentic data, together with the known facts of Washington's visits to Philadelphia and the deep personal interest he took in the flag question, checks fully with Betsy's account of the time and circumstances of the birth of Old Glory in June, 1776. For over fifty years thereafter, she continued to make flags, assisted as time passed by her oldest daughter and a niece. This occupation began with the Washington interview and succeeded the upholstery business in which she started her married life.

The writer remembers many times hearing his grandfather, Edwin Satterthwaite, who was one of her grandsons and for some years a member of the Pennsylvania legislature, a man of keen mind and clear recollection, speak of his visits at her home when a youth; of the quantities of red, white, and blue bunting all about the little shop, and of her sending him out to Eighth Street, then at the city's outskirts, "to pick blackberries for luncheon." He was eighteen years old when she died. Left-over pieces of flag bunting he often took out to his mother, one of Betsy's daughters living in the near-by township of Abington, and later on, to his wife—for making rag carpets. The fragments of pure wool, brightly colored, were excellent for that purpose. Many a doll's dress was also made of them by the children of the household.

Betsy Ross left no letters or writings bearing on her life or the making of the first flag. Letter writing among our ancestors was much less frequent than it is today. The mail and travel routes were hazardous and uncertain. One's friends, for the most part, lived near at hand, and communication with others was confined largely to visits or to brief messages carried by mutual acquaintances.

The making of a flag was not a tremendously important event to her at the time. She was young. Its significance was swallowed up in the rush of weightier events all about her. The records of Congress, Washington's diary, and other Revolutionary writings are also lacking in information as to how the Stars and Stripes originated. Betsy herself did not record it. But later she stated her part in it as a simple fact. And the word of this sincere and trustworthy Quakeress has become one of America's most treasured traditions. It is recognized that the basis of the history of any event is the spoken or written word of some individual or individuals.

The most exhaustive work yet published on the history and development of the American Flag was that by Rear Admiral George H. Preble, U. S. N., in 1872. He states that his investigation covered a period of twenty years and that he examined over a thousand documents and manuscripts. He mentions the Betsy Ross explanation of the flag's origin from a design supplied to her by General Washington. While unable to verify it except by the statements attributed to her, he found no other record of the actual conception of the Star-spangled Banner to supplant it.

Most of the facts about the early use of the flag and where it was carried in battle are lost in the dim vistas of time. It is even questioned that it was carried to any great extent in the Revolution by the land forces—only on the sea.

Preble declares, on the contrary, that without doubt it waved at Brandywine, Germantown, and Valley Forge—possibly earlier. He and other writers refer to the paintings of Peale and Trumbull, soldiers of the Revolution, as interesting testimony. While further evidence of the flag's use in the field and over forts is seen in several old banners which have been preserved, correspondence between the Board of War and Washington indicate it was not officially specified for the land forces until later. Apparently it was confined principally to the navy, with which he was as deeply concerned as with the army.

Interest in the origin of Old Glory and the lady who first fashioned it seems to increase year by year with the growth of the country and the spread of its influence. Rear Admiral Richard E. Byrd, U. S. N., whose polar flights have planted the Stars and Stripes at both the top and bottom of the world, made a third historic airplane journey from New York to France in 1927. In a specially made compartment in a wing of his plane, "America," he carried an object of unusual interest— a strip of the bunting used long ago in the Betsy Ross flag-making shop. Rodman Wanamaker, who sponsored the flight, had secured the rare fragment a short time before the start, from Miss Anne Balderston, one of Betsy's great grand-daughters, residing in Maryland.

"As a gift to the French republic from Mr. Wanamaker, we carried the bunting as one of our most precious relics," said Commander Byrd in his narrative of the flight published by the National Geographic Society, which had coöperat-ed with him in charting his expedition.   And when the giant airship, with fuel exhausted in the fog, came crashing down into the waters of Ver-sur-Mer, on the coast of France, the first thought of Byrd and his comrades was of that little com-partment and its priceless contents.

To piece together the facts that are known about Betsy Ross and her relationship to the events amid which she lived is the object of this book—a brief biography in story form.   She has often been pic-tured as an obscure, middle-aged seamstress upon whom a committee chanced to call for assistance in the making of the flag.   The real Betsy Ross was a charming young woman in her early twenties, with originality and ingenuity.   She never laid claim to designing the flag. However, but for her insistence, it would probably have had six-pointed stars instead of five-pointed.

The early records of the Society of Friends, genealogical records of families involved, and a much treasured journal written by one of her lovers in an English prison, and still in the possession of her descendants, form much of the basis of the following chapters. Interwoven with it are facts from old documents bearing on the Revolution and scenes in its pivotal city.

Betsy Ross was definitely a part of the Philadelphia of long ago—of Penn's city with its Quaker charm, into which the war and its turmoil so ruthlessly entered. She just as definitely represented the spirit which animated the new nation in its fight for freedom. In the old quarter of the city where met the Continental Congress, there are many places of historic interest. Chief among them is Independence Hall, and after that the Betsy Ross House, maintained by the American Flag House and Betsy Ross Memorial Association. Increasing hosts of visitors are attracted each year to these scenes of two memorable events—the birth of freedom and the birth of the flag.

2

During the recent World War, this was emphasized in a striking manner. It was noted that American soldiers passing through Philadelphia on their way overseas were particularly eager to visit the Flag House. As each group filed with bared heads reverently into the room where the first American flag was made, it was a thrilling and impressive scene and one that bore eloquent testimony to the depth and sincerity of the nation's patriotism.

Acknowledgments

of indebtedness by the author are made to the following:

Pennsylvania, Colony and Commonwealth, by Sydney George Fisher; *Watson's Annals of Philadelphia; The Friends' Meeting House,* by Isaac Sharpless and others; *Early Quaker Education in Pennsylvania,* by Thomas Woody; *The American Revolution,* by John Fiske; *Life of Washington,* by Washington Irving; *Paintings by John Trumbull at Yale University,* by John Hill Morgan; *Evolution of the American Flag* by George Canby and Lloyd Balderston; *Our Flag,* by Rear Admiral George H. Preble, U. S. N.; and other works by students of flag history. Also to authors of genealogies named in the Appendix.

My special thanks are due to Lloyd Balderston, Ph.D., a great grandson of Betsy Ross, whose writings and whose familiarity with her life were valuable guidance; to officers of the American Flag House and Betsy Ross Memorial Association, for their coöperation; and to the Historical Society of Pennsylvania, the Public Library of New York, the Free Library of Riverton, New Jersey, the Custodians of Records of the Society of Friends, in Philadelphia, and those in charge of the old records of the Society of the Free Quakers, for so courteously placing their books and archives at my disposal.

I

A Daughter of the Revolution

A YOUNG woman, sweet-faced, but with blue eyes that flashed indifference to the charge against her, sat in her small living room confronting an austere committee of men and women in Quaker garb. Their spokesman solemnly read a document which disowned her from the faith her fathers had espoused for generations.

Disgrace was her portion, in accordance with Quaker law, for having given her heart to a youth of another religious persuasion.

Two years later, this same young woman, now widowed by a tragedy of the Revolution, sat in the same room one June morning listening to another and very different committee. Its spokesman was General Washington, who sought her aid in fashioning an ensign for the Continental ships and army.

Outside the tiny brick dwelling, Philadelphia was throbbing with war activity. Four blocks away, in the old State House, a body of serious gentlemen in knee breeches and pigtails were wrestling with the problems of national defense. King George's army and fleet were knocking at the doors of New York—with the city of Penn scheduled next on their busy program.

Excited men fill the streets. The air is charged with forebodings and terrifying rumors. Independence is being heatedly discussed in pamphlets and in the taverns. The Virginia delegates to Congress are urging complete separation from the Crown as an absolute necessity—and Washington, a year ago so opposed to the idea, has now declared, "I am fully convinced that nothing else will save us."

But such a bold and dangerous course, he sees, will require a far larger army and more ships. It will demand a closer union of the colonies. "We must all hang together," as Doctor Franklin put it a few weeks later, "or we shall all hang separately." Had not the British general, Gage, declared that the rebel leaders taken prisoner at Bunker Hill were all "destined to the cord"?

And among a thousand other needs, the patriot commander sees that a declaration of freedom will require the adoption of a national flag for the new nation—a definite symbol for his men to fight for, on land and sea.

* * * * * *

It all seemed so incongruous that Betsy Griscom, daughter of Samuel and Rebecca Griscom, should be so mixed up with military matters—and forbidden love affairs.

As far back as they could be traced, her ancestors had been arrayed on the side of sobriety and peace and those virtues which made up the strict code of the Friends. Andrew Griscom, her great-grandfather, had come to America before William Penn himself—and had been one of his stanchest supporters in the founding of a different sort of colony, in which all forms of strife and discord were to be looked upon as coldly as worldly pleasures.

And now, in the fourth generation of the Griscoms in America, there came a demure but headstrong maiden who seemed to delight in upsetting these traditions and allying herself with ideas which her forbears discountenanced.

Almost from her school days, when her good looks started to attract attention, Betsy Griscom had revealed notions that disturbed her Quaker relatives. And as the war clouds began to darken the heavens, her rebellious ways seemed to grow in the same proportion, and bear her toward the "iniquitous" and fateful marriage which made her Betsy Ross. From the date of that union, both tragedy and romance seemed to pursue her.

A rebel in a double sense was this young woman who is known to the world as Betsy Ross. Revolting against Quaker tradition in her first love affair—and succeeding love affairs—she took an equally decided stand against her mother country when the issue came. In a hotbed of Toryism she was one of the first to side with the rebel cause, and she was cast in the rôle of flag maker quite largely as a result of her first forbidden marriage and her patriotic zeal.

Betsy Ross, who put together the first banner of Stars and Stripes, as a legendary figure is familiar to every schoolboy and girl in America. But the story of Betsy Ross, daughter of the Revolution, and her experiences through the seven years of conflict, has remained untold. Apart from the incident which brought her fame, it envelops with interest extraordinary the quaint little Flag House where Old Glory was born.

II

The Builders

WHEN Penn's first shiploads of colonists came up the Delaware late in the fall of 1681 and picked out the site for Philadelphia on a "high, wide, and pleasant plain," the immediate necessity was to find shelter for the winter.

There were forests all about them, abounding in game—which largely answered the food question—and with trees of every description. But the settlers had no sawmills. Neither did they have bricks and mortar.

So, as the first step in the founding of the city, they proceeded to dig themselves into the steep bank of the river. For half a mile along the water's edge there soon stretched a village of caves, roofed, in part, with sod and bark and rushes. Farther back, log cabins sprang up as the broadax gradually ate its way into the timber toward the Schuylkill. The largest of these cabins was the Meeting House, and the next to the largest was the school.

The business of building was an important one, and would be for some time to come—and to it Andrew Griscom devoted his energies. This Quaker pioneer had come from England to the province of West Jersey the year before, and now cast his lot with the followers of Penn. For his own estate, the old records tell us, he took out a patent for four hundred ninety-five acres of land in Pennsylvania, north of what is now the Spring Garden district. By so large a purchase he became entitled, in addition, to a town lot within the city proper. At a "council held on the twenty-fourth day of the Twelfth month, 1683," the records state, "Andrew Grifcom was put upon the firſt Grand Jury, William Penn being preſent."

Soon the log cabins and caves disappeared as shiploads of bricks came from the mother country. And then—to the joy of all—the soil of the new colony was found to have rich substrata of clay! The building of the city leaped forward in row upon row of brick dwellings and shops, three hundred houses coming into existence within a period of two years. And the streets were named, for the most part, for the trees of the forests.

The very first brick house in Philadelphia had been built by Andrew Griscom, and many others after it. So well did he prosper at his trade that Tobias, his son, and Samuel, his grandson, father of the flag maker, followed in his footsteps, and when, as the years passed, the leading house carpenters of the city formed a guild for their mutual benefit and instruction in architecture, we find Tobias and Samuel among the early members. On the wall of the assembly room in historic Carpenters' Hall, where met the first Continental Congress, their names are still recorded. Later on this famous guild was incorporated as the Carpenters' Company, Samuel Griscom being one of those to bring that action about. In 1751 he helped to erect the belfry of Independence Hall, completed some years after the main building.

There are still standing near the river front in old Philadelphia, shops and dwellings built by Tobias and Samuel Griscom, their thick walls, their black-oak joists, their hand-split lath and hand-forged nails testifying why they have so well withstood the flight of time.

But if the building of buildings was important to the colony's growth, the rearing of families

was even more so. In 1742 Samuel Griscom took
to wife one Rebecca James, and moved into the
substantial residence in Arch Street, turned over
to him by his father, who had, in the meantime,
bought and occupied lands in Jersey. Rebecca,
descendant of an old Quaker family, was a sister
of Abel James, of the commission house firm of
James and Drinker, at whose beck and call ships
brought merchandise from all quarters of the globe.

Those were days of large families, and that of
Samuel and Rebecca Griscom proved no exception
to the rule. Seventeen children were born to
them, nine of whom—eight girls and a boy, the
latter the youngest—lived to maturity. The
seventh daughter to bless their union was Elizabeth—she whose name destiny had so strangely
singled out to live in history.

*   *   *   *   *   *

Arch Street, Philadelphia, begins at the Delaware River, and after a sharp rise where the cave
dwellers had made their homes, runs westward,
with occasional breaks, for approximately seven
miles. Up to the time of the Revolution, there
were few houses west of Eighth Street, a scant mile
from the river, all beyond that being open country.

Today it is lined with warehouses and factory buildings and resounds with the din of trucks and trolley cars; but in those times it was a quiet, village-like thoroughfare flanked by rows of linden trees and the modest homes of Quaker families. Originally called Mulberry Street, the name was changed to Arch because of an arch or bridge for traffic built over its depression at the river edge.

Near the corner of Fourth and Mulberry Streets, Betsy Griscom was born on New Year's Day, 1752. Less than two blocks from her home, toward the Delaware, was the little brick dwelling into which one day she was to move as a bride, and which is today a national shrine—the birthplace of the flag. To the southward one block was Market or High Street, the main thoroughfare of the town, with its market place and court house, its taverns and fine residences, while just beyond was Chestnut Street and the old State House, later famed as Independence Hall.

That year, 1752, was full of interesting events. In June, Doctor Benjamin Franklin, flying a kite from his spacious garden at Second and Race Streets, a few squares from the Griscom home, proved that lightning and electricity are identical.

Then he startled the scientific world and shocked the clergy by enticing thunderbolts earthward through what thousands of God-fearing people termed his "satanic device," the lightning rod. It was a time of the rapid progress of science in a world filled with religious fervor.

In August of that year in which Elizabeth Griscom came on the scene, there was another arrival of high importance to the city's future—the great new bell for the State House tower. Cast in London on order by the Pennsylvania Assembly, and weighing 2080 pounds, it was unloaded from a ship in the Delaware, carted up Chestnut Street and exhibited and tested in the State House yard before being lifted to the belfry.

But Betsy Griscom, oblivious of such marvels and such discussions, grew into sturdy childhood. Very early in the life of every Quaker came two important influences—School and Meeting. And soon we find the little Elizabeth trudging down Arch Street each morning toward the shining river, and just before she reached it, turning into Drinker's Alley. For there, at Number 8, lived Rebecca Jones who conducted a school for the very young children of Quaker households, with the capable Hannah Cathrall acting as her assistant. Hannah Cathrall, capable indeed, but rigid in discipline—the same who in a later year, was to lead the way in evicting Betsy Griscom from the Quaker fold!

From the very beginning of their colony, the Friends had encouraged establishment of schools in connection with their Meetings. That of Rebecca Jones was held in special favor, for long had she been a prominent figure both as teacher and preacher. Each Sabbath she sat among the elders at the Bank Meeting House on the river bank at Front and Arch Streets, close by, where the Friends had worshiped ever since 1684.

THE HORSE FERRY DOCKED AT THE FOOT OF HIGH STREET
(NOW CALLED MARKET STREET)

One cold morning in February, 1762, a chronicler of the period relates, John Woolman, a noted minister and writer from Mount Holly, New Jersey, who was in Philadelphia attending the Friends' Quarterly Meeting, "rofe early after a heavy fnow ftorm and with a fhovel made a good footway for the ladies all the way to the Bank Meeting Houfe. After breakfaft, he made another path for the entrance of Rebecca Jones's pupils to her fchool."

That same winter, in which Elizabeth Griscom rounded out her first decade of existence, was an exceptionally bitter one. Sleighs and ox teams bringing the country Friends to Quarterly Meeting had all they could do to get through the drifts, and the New Jersey Friends experienced even greater difficulty because of the ice which choked the mile-wide river and made it hazardous for the horse ferry to navigate. This usually reliable ferry, which docked at the foot of High Street, consisted of a large flatboat propelled by a rear paddle wheel—said paddle wheel being operated by a capstan in the center of the boat, turned by four sturdy horses. At the mild seasons of the year, when traffic was heaviest, two of these craft were kept constantly busy.

III

The Rule of the Rod

FROM the reading, 'riting, 'rithmetic stage
under Rebecca Jones and Hannah Cathrall,
Betsy followed her older sisters to the larger
Friends' Public School in South Fourth Street
below Chestnut, which admitted pupils of all religious denominations. This important institution
of old-time Philadelphia was one of those set up
at Penn's order and chartered as "Public Grammar
Schools" so that "proper care might be taken
about the learning and inftruction of youth."
It was attended by boys and girls of the wealthy
classes as well as by those in moderate circumstances. Many members of the Morris, Shippen,
Biddle, Pemberton, Mifflin, and other families
prominent in the Councils of Pennsylvania, received their education there.

Going to school was a serious business in colonial
times. Betsy and her friends were expected to be in
their places sharply at eight o'clock in the morning by the State House clock, which was clearly

visible from the school windows. They studied
and recited until six in the evening, with a break of
two hours at noon when they usually went home
for dinner. Both boys and girls were required to
spend much time in tasks leading up to their life
work, as is indicated by the following routine laid
down for Quaker schools:

That the fcholars be kept in the morning two
hours at reading, writing, bookkeeping, etc., and
two hours at work in that art, myftery or trade
that he or fhe moft delighteth in, and then let them
have two hours to dine, and for recreation and in
the afternoon two hours at reading, writing, etc.,
and the other two hours at work at their feveral
employments.

The feventh day of the week the fcholars may
come to fchool only in the forenoon, and at a certain hour in the afternoon let a meeting be kept
by the fchoolmafters and their fcholars where good
inftruction and admonition is given by the mafters
to the fcholars and thanks returned to the Lord
for his mercies and bleffings that are daily received
from Him, then let a ftrict examination be made
by the mafters, of the converfation of the fcholars
in the week paft, and let reproof, admonition and
correction be given to the offenders, according to
the quantity and quality of their faults.

As often as not, this admonition and correction of offenders took the form of the birch or the strap, freely administered—and, if the truth must be told, to young ladies as well as to young gentlemen. Such disciplinary measures were, as the masters claimed, one of their most important contributions to good citizenship. The thoroughgoing methods of one of these masters, J. Todd by name, are vividly pictured by a celebrated annalist of old Philadelphia:

He, Todd, dressed after the plainest manner of Friends, but of the richest material, with looped cocked hat, was a man of about sixty years, square built and well sustained by bone and muscle.

After an hour, maybe, of quiet time, everything going smoothly on—no sound but from the master's voice, while hearing the one standing near him—a dead calm—when suddenly a brisk slap on the ear or face for something or nothing, gave dreadful note that an irruption of the lava was about to take place. The chair would be quickly thrust on one side, when, with sudden grip, he was to be seen dragging his struggling suppliant to the flogging ground in the center of the room. Having placed his left foot upon the end of a bench, he then, with a patent jerk, peculiar to himself, would have the boy completely horsed across his knee,

with his left elbow on the back of his neck, to
keep him squarely on.   In the hurry of the moment, he would bring his long pen with him,
gripped between his strong teeth, causing the both
ends to descend to a parallel with his chin, and
adding much to the terror of the scene.

Having his victim thus completely at command,
and all useless drapery drawn up to a bunch above
the waistband, then to the "staring crew" would
be exhibited the dexterity of master and strap.
By long practice he had arrived at such perfection
in the exercise, that, moving in quick time, the fifteen inches of bridle rein (alias strap) would be
seen, after every cut, elevated like a flail, leaving
on the place beneath a fiery red streak at every
slash.   It was customary with him to address the
sufferer at intervals, "Does it hurt?"   ("O! yes,
master, O! don't, master.")   "Then I'll make it
hurt thee more.   I'll make thy flesh creep.   Thou
shan't want a warming pan tonight—intolerable
being!   Nothing in nature is able to prevail upon
thee but my strap."

"The girls too—we pity them!" states the annalist, "were obliged to take off their stays to
receive their floggings with equal sensibility."

But this was quite in line with the custom of
meting out corporal punishment to all evildoers

of the time. On Wednesday and Saturday, which were high market days, when farm wagons stood thick along the curbs, laden with products of the soil, the grist mill and the hand butter churn, Elizabeth Griscom and her schoolmates often witnessed the public flogging of both men and women at Third and High Streets. For there, at the west end of the market, only a few yards from the book shop and print shop of the estimable Doctor Franklin, stood the pillory and the whipping post on a raised platform. And to add to the humiliating plight of the law's victims, they were usually paraded through the streets beforehand, headed by the town crier in order to draw a crowd. Then, with arms pinioned and clothes stripped to the waist and backs bleeding from the strokes of the lash, they stood through their punishment in plain view of all who chose to look.

It is not recorded whether Betsy Griscom was a model pupil, or when she completed her schooling. The years passed rapidly and pleasantly for the light-hearted girl despite the straight and narrow path along which Quaker youths and maidens were accustomed to tread. At the home of Samuel Griscom, the principles of the Society of Friends were observed in their strictest sense. Worldly amusements were discountenanced. There was no music or dancing or card playing such as enlivened the more elaborate homes of the fashionable folk at the upper ends of Walnut and Spruce Streets, and on "Society Hill." Novels were frowned upon, and the Sabbath was a day when one must read nothing but the Bible.

"Parents fhould be exemplary to their children in Converfation, and in keeping out of the vain Fafhions, Cuftoms and Pride of the World, by adorning themfelves modeftly and in Plainnefs,"

said the old Book of Discipline or Catechism of the Friends. And Samuel and Rebecca Griscom took good care that in the rearing of their brood there should be little grounds for criticism on that score.

Equal care was bestowed upon their training toward usefulness. The Quaker religion abhorred idleness, and from early childhood the Griscom sisters were drilled in the daily tasks which would make of them practical and capable housewives— or perhaps breadwinners should occasion demand.

Thrifty homes in those days made their own clothing, even spinning the yarn and weaving the cloth, and there were few maidens more skilled in such matters than those in the Griscom household. Betsy, at an early age, drew attention to herself by her fine needlework, which gave free play to her individuality and became the talk of the neighborhood. At school exhibits and at the High Street fairs where such handiwork was shown, she more than once carried off honors.

But there is ample evidence that the thoughts of this Griscom daughter were not always fixed on household tasks or even upon the simple pleasures countenanced by her faith. As she approached young womanhood, Betsy grew in comeliness—and to a degree which soon brought concern to her parents—for they found it causing fully as much talk through the neighborhood as her needleworked samplers so beautifully done in silk and golden thread—though among a different group.

Not that they objected to physical perfection in itself, but they discovered that she was growing conscious of her charm and was exercising it to an extent scarcely in keeping with the piety of a daughter of the Quakers.

A widening circle of young men began to take an interest in Betsy Griscom and to bask in the sunlight of pretty smiles and a sprightly conversation which lifted her personality above the ordinary. She plainly enjoyed their company, and much to the annoyance of Samuel Griscom, he saw that those who called at her home or who joined step with hers as she went upon her shopping errands or her visits to the meat and vegetable market in High Street, were not all of the plain speech or plain attire which betokened the consistent Friend. Both her ways and her talk they found beguiling. It was a sweet novelty to be addressed as "thee," with the word coming from such pretty lips.

Moreover, it is said that when the Griscom family walked down Arch Street to the Bank Meeting First Day mornings, determined youths of the "other side," as the church members were termed, were known to wait in the meetinghouse yard until Betsy had entered with her parents. Occasionally one bolder than the rest would actually follow and seat himself on one of the severely plain, unpainted benches where he could have a clear view of the devout young lady and speculate on his chances of escorting her home.

The quaint attire of the maidens of the Quaker sect, with white bonnets framing their sweet faces,

Determined Youths Waited for Betsy at the Meeting House Yard

seemed to have a lure in itself for those of the opposite sex, and especially, it seems, for those of opposite faiths.

"Ah," writes a Friend of long ago, "if one could only describe those white, plain bonnets. I used to sit at my uncle's front window when a boy to watch them. Arch Street was lined with them as the young women hurried by to meeting. I could almost fancy them to be gleaming white lilies, seeming to bend and sway like lily stalks in the breeze as their wearers nodded to friends or chatted together. No wonder that the street boys sometimes ran on ahead and then faced about to catch a glimpse of some especially fair girlish face in its pure framing. The gayer New Jersey girls had sometimes a hint of pink coloring, like the arbutus of their own woods."

IV

The Rivals

OF the many young men who showed diligent interest in Betsy Griscom, three in particular were ardent suitors for her hand: Joseph Ashburn, ship captain; John Claypoole, son of William Claypoole, tanner; and John Ross, an upholsterer's apprentice.

All three lived in the vicinity of her home and were members of the crowd of young people who had known her through her school days and had romped together as children at tag or town ball— or with marbles and tops on the Arch Street flagstones. The lives of these three, closely mingled from boyhood, were destined to be interwoven with her own—and to run tragic courses during the dark days of the Revolution so near at hand.

None of the trio was a member of the Society of Friends, though John Claypoole came of an old and prominent Quaker family, and on that account Betsy's parents and the elders of the Meeting probably viewed him with the least disfavor of the three.

Joseph Ashburn sailed a merchant vessel owned
by his aunt, the well-to-do widow Ashburn who
lived in Front Street. His voyages to the West
Indies for cargoes of cotton, sugar, spices, and
tobacco kept him from home for weeks at a time.
This was a serious handicap in a competition for a
maiden's heart. And the fact that his ship was
sometimes heavily laden with casks of fine Jamaica
rum did not help his case any with her parents.

John Ross was under a worse handicap still,
though of a different sort. He was the son of an
Episcopal clergyman, the Rev. Aneas Ross, at one
time assistant rector of the stately Christ Church
in Second Street. From the standpoint of Betsy's
father and mother, this was enough to eliminate
him completely as a candidate for her hand. Not
only were marriages with persons of other denominations, in those days, strictly forbidden by the
Meeting, but hired clergy were an anathema to
the Society of Friends.

The religious affiliations of her suitors apparently
worried this independent young lady but little,
however, and less as time went on. In the merry
groups which came together on outings or in
neighborhood affairs, she showed no prejudice on

that account. In fact, if we are to judge by events, her preference was in the opposite direction from that which her training would lead one to expect.

The young people of colonial Philadelphia did not lack opportunity for recreation and wholesome fun. Picnics into the Governor's woods along the then romantic and picturesque banks of the Schuylkill River, or out into the country districts toward Germantown, Chestnut Hill, or Frankford, inevitably brought the youthful Quakers and the "church members" into each other's society. Sailing parties on the upper Delaware to Burlington or Bordentown were popular through the summer, and during the old-fashioned winters the river surfaces were filled with skaters.

There were other pastimes, however, not so harmless, upon which the Friends frowned with great severity. Out Race Street, near what is now Thirteenth Street, where the Governor's woods began, was a race track which acted as a magnet Saturday afternoons. The reports of horse racing and gambling at high stakes which regularly reached their ears caused the overseers of the Meeting to regard it as a blight upon the city.

To add to their concern, the place was known to be a rendezvous for cockfighting, which attracted youths of weak moral fiber, and, what was worse, bull baiting. This cruel sport brought the largest and wildest animals which cattle raisers drove to town, into deadly combat with bulldogs.

In the evenings, these same misguided youths idled away their time at the London Coffee Shop at the foot of High Street, or at the Bag of Nails, the Crooked Billet, and other drinking places along the river front, which, as a consequence, were favorite topics for denunciation at the Bank Meeting and at the Great Meeting House at Second and High Streets when Friends discussed their own and the community's welfare.

Elizabeth Griscom had no leanings toward young men of questionable tendencies. Her parents did not need to worry about that side of her character. What gave them their chief anxiety was her failure, in the competition for her favor, to draw the line between Quakers and outsiders as all dutiful maidens were expected to do. Whether from a spirit of mischief or a growing feeling of revolt against too much shaping of the lives of herself and her sisters, she seemed to take a special delight

in inviting the admiration of those who did not
wear the broad-brimmed hats and the drab garb
with which she had been surrounded all her days.

To Samuel Griscom, a matter-of-fact, unreason-
ing man, whose word had always been law in his
household, this perversity was an enigma he could
not fathom. As time went on, reports reached him
that Betsy was being seen more and more frequently in the company of John Ross, whose
infatuation for the lovely Quaker girl seemed to
be sweeping aside all rivals. Many serious discussions between father and daughter resulted.
He gave her plainly to understand that such meetings must not continue, lest they lead to disaster.

But the woodland lanes winding toward the
Schuylkill and the shaded bank of the quiet flow-
ing Delaware north of the city were attractive
settings for moonlight strolls—so alluring evidently
that parental commands were completely out-
weighed. Especially since the young woman in
the case was unusually strong-willed and took the
position that where perfect love existed, objection
on religious grounds was no objection at all.

Betsy found herself drawn irresistibly toward
the tall, good-looking clergyman's son, met him

where and when she could—and if human nature was the same in olden times as now, the secrecy occasioned by disapproval at home only added to the excitement of the trysts. All day John was at work at the shop of William Webster in Second Street below Chestnut, learning the upholsterer's trade. A convenient place they found that also for daytime chats. How many times Betsy, on her market errands, thrust her pretty head into the shop doorway, seeking to purloin a few precious moments from her lover's busy day, particularly in Friend William's absence, no one now knows.

Thus their affair proceeded until one day, nerving herself for the ordeal that must be gone through with, she suddenly informed her family that she had promised to marry John Ross. John himself was not present. She preferred to handle the matter alone.

Quietly spoken was her announcement, but an earthquake could have caused no greater commotion. The consternation of her parents was none the less for having lived in dread of just such news. For a moment Samuel Griscom looked at his daughter as though he could not believe his ears.

Was the girl out of her mind?

She made it plain that she was perfectly sane. There followed then a stormy scene the like of which had never taken place in that placid household before. The father's face blazed with anger.

Did she understand the full meaning of her conduct, he demanded. Did she realize that she would be in disgrace among Friends, that she would be an outcast from the Meeting?

To which Betsy calmly replied that she had carefully considered these things, and while she deeply regretted them, her mind was fully made up.

Did she realize she was about to bring shame and humiliation upon her family?

She understood that, too, but she could not help it.

Her mother's tearful pleading was likewise to no avail. Betsy's face was troubled but determined. The parents, unused to grappling with such problems, and living by a code which they held sacred, saw that code now being toppled by a wilful and disobedient daughter—helpless to prevent it. For there was that in her eyes and manner which told them further argument was useless.

The elders of the Meeting were equally shocked. Was it not to get away from the forms and dogmas of the Church of England that the Quakers had come to America a century before? Yet here was one of their number about to ally herself with one of the most conspicuous families in that faith.

In the present more liberal age, it is difficult for us to understand the denominational tension of that period. Groups which had left England primarily to seek freedom of worship, showed but little tolerance for other beliefs. In the early colonies, the church was the center of things in each community. The Puritans in New England even made membership in their church a qualification for public office—and public meetings were often held in the church. In Pennsylvania, community interests centered about the Meeting House, and though Quakerism was in no way a condition of officeholding, the government was kept strictly in the hands of the Friends long after Penn arrived as Proprietor of the lands deeded to him by the king. Gradually the members of other sects, drawn there in numbers by the colony's prosperity, came to share in the government. For some years prior to the Revolution they actually dominated it. But while it was a fixed Quaker law to mistreat no one because of

4

religious belief, the ban against intermarriage remained until a long time afterward. Feeling
between the Friends and Episcopalians was particularly acute, since the latter had taken a leading part
in wresting legislative control from the followers of
Penn. It was largely an outgrowth of friction dating from the Indian wars when Quakers had been
held up to ridicule because of refusal to bear arms.

But aside from these things, there was the
serious Quaker view of marriage itself. It was
not simply a contract, it was a religion, which
required utmost unity of thought and faith for
true happiness to result. Hence the barrier which
they set up between themselves and other sects
and the severe penalty for breaking it down.

There are no letters or diaries, either of John
Ross or his sweetheart, in existence to tell us of
their wooing, or of the young man's joy at con-
quering the obstacles in his path. One needs no
such records, however, to picture his state of mind.

From what has been handed down to us through
her family and others who knew her, Betsy Griscom, at twenty, was without a doubt one of the
most attractive young women in the province of
Pennsylvania. She was of medium height. Her

blue eyes had a luster full of intelligence and spirit. Her hair was a rich chestnut brown, her cheeks warm with color. With her engaging manner, she combined a positiveness which made her a leader among her girlhood friends and in after life. One of the things most remembered about her was her fund of ready wit, the shafts of which, directed at current foibles and personages, often shocked while they amused her staid Quaker relatives.

John Ross, quiet, serious-minded, was by temperament a marked contrast to the maiden he had chosen to be his wife. Like the families of most clergymen, his parents were blessed with very little of this world's goods; hence the necessity of his starting out at an early age to earn a livelihood. Hardly was he through school when he was apprenticed to William Webster to learn the art of covering and finishing chairs and sofas. What the Reverend Ross thought of his love affair we do not know, though the Episcopalians had none of the strictness of the Quakers on the subject of intermarriage.

As the months wore on, Samuel and Rebecca Griscom renewed their efforts to deter their daughter from her unwise alliance.

Mixing in Marriage with thofe not of our Profeffion is an unequal Yoking which brings ill Confequence to the Parties as well as Grief to their honeft Friends and Relatives, and frequently ends in Woe and Ruin of themfelves and their Children.

Thus read the Book of Discipline, and for such marriage disownment by the Society was the penalty. Often it meant disownment by the family as well.

At the request of her worried parents, influential Friends called upon Betsy and labored with her, but in vain.

"I love John Ross, and I will marry him whatever happens," was her simple rejoinder.

There was nothing to do, therefore, but to bow to the inevitable, and await the Meeting's action should she carry out her purpose.

Little did this young woman or her lover or her parents think that in her determined stand, which was to bring her disgrace in Quaker eyes, she was paving the way for her part in another and important event which was to give her lasting fame, and associate her name forever with the romance of her country's flag.

V

The Disownment

THE year 1773 was one long remembered in the American provinces. For in that year a mounting unpleasantness with Great Britain, seething and rumbling along the Atlantic seaboard, began to boil over. In fact, love and reverence for the mother country gave way almost completely to hatred and ridicule.

Long before, in the days when Betsy Griscom was a little girl in school, the weak and youthful King George III had begun to make himself unpopular. She could remember, at thirteen, hearing people, even the Quakers, angrily discussing the Stamp Act, under which nobody could make a will or buy a newspaper or publish a pamphlet unless it bore a stamp purchased from agents of the British government. Patrick Henry, in a fiery speech in Virginia, and other wrathful citizens had stirred up such a commotion against this method of taking money from their pockets that the Act was hastily repealed.

But the British treasury needed replenishing as a result of foreign wars, and the king and his ministers took the position that the first duty of all colonists was to be useful and submissive to the mother country. So taxes were put back—this time in the form of heavy duties on tea, glass, lead, paper, and other imported things everyone had to use every day of his life. And furthermore, when the colonists asked for representation in Parliament, they were laughed at.

In Boston one day British soldiers clashed with a group of angry townsfolk in the streets, killing five of them—and now in the latter part of 1773, Philadelphians heard new and sensational reports from Massachusetts where the rebellious feeling was hottest. A self-appointed committee of young men, disguised as Indians, had boarded His Majesty's tea ships in Boston harbor under cover of darkness, had broken open the tea chests with tomahawks and tossed the costly contents overboard. No less than 18,000 pounds sterling were thus lost to British merchants.

In the taverns along High and Front Streets in the Quaker City, where men came together for grog and political talk, this news was received

with loud acclaim, and many a toast was drunk
to the Bostonians who dared to stage the Tea
Party. Similar measures, indeed, were already
brewing against tea ships coming up the Delaware,
with tar and feathering to boot, for the British
skippers. But over in the Arch Street community
of Friends, such things were heard with much
shaking of heads. They admitted their country's
wrongs, but they could not countenance the waste-
fulness and violence.

Into Betsy Griscom's own family circle, however, the "deteftable tea" question was now suddenly thrust—and with startling developments
which threatened to cause a tea party even more
drastic than the one in Boston.

It happened that her uncle, Abel James, head
of the importing firm of James and Drinker, had
ignored the popular clamor against the tea ships.
A stern and inflexible Quaker, master of his own
affairs, he persisted in carrying on business as
usual. It also happened that a rich cargo of tea
consigned to James and Drinker was then on its
way across the ocean in the British brig *Polly*,
under Captain Ayres, and that this fact became
noised about.

One day a large printed card was delivered at Mr. James's office in Front Street, at the corner of Black Horse Alley, and copies of it were found nailed to the doorways of neighboring warehouses.

A CARD

The PUBLIC prefents their compliments to Meffieurs James and Drinker. We are informed that you have this Day received your Commiffion to enslave your Native Country; and as your frivolous Plea of having received no Advice relative to the fcandalous Part you were to act in the TEA Scheme can no longer ferve your Purpofe nor divert our Attention, we expect and defire you will immediately inform the PUBLIC by a Line or two to be left at the COFFEE HOUSE, whether you will not renounce all Pretenfions to execute that Commiffion. We will govern ourfelves accordingly.

The news of this extraordinary document, which was unsigned, flew about the city. With astonishment and perturbation, it must have been received at the home of Samuel Griscom, as well as at those of Messrs. James and Drinker. We do not know what Betsy's attitude in the family discussion was, but if we can judge from her patriotic make-up in general, she did *not* agree with her mother's brother.

The warning to James and Drinker, however, was mild compared to the message addressed to Captain Ayres. This took the form of a handbill prepared by a so-called "Committee for Tar and Feathering," copies of which were supplied to Delaware River pilots to give to the skipper as soon as he should put in an appearance.

To Capt. Ayres

We are informed that you have, impudently, taken Charge of a Quantity of TEA, which has been fent out by the India Company under the aufpices of the Miniftry, as a Trial of American Virtue and Refolution.

Now as your Cargo, on your Arrival here, will most affuredly bring you into hot water; and as you are perhaps a Stranger to thefe parts, we have concluded to advife you of the prefent fituation of affairs in Philadelphia—that, taking Time by the Forelock, you may ftop fhort in your dangerous Errand—fecure your Ship againft the Rafts of combuftible Matter which may be fet on Fire, and turned loofe againft her; and more than all this, that you may preferve your own Perfon from the Pitch and Feathers that are prepared for you. . . .

You are fent out on a diabolical Service; and if you are fo foolifh and obftinate as to compleat your Voyage, by bringing your Ship to Anchor in this Port; you may run fuch a Gauntlet as will induce you in your laft moments, moft heartily to curfe thofe who have made you the Dupe of their Avarice and Ambition.

What think you, Captain, of a Halter around your neck—ten Gallons of liquid Tar decanted on your Pate—with the feathers of a dozen wild Geefe laid over that to enliven your appearance?

Only think ferioufly of this—and fly to the Place from whence you came—fly without Hefitation—without the Formality of a Proteft—and above all, Captain Ayres, let us advife you to fly without the wild geefe Feathers.

(Signed)   Your Friends to ferve,
The Committee for Tar and Feathering—

Philadelphia, Nov. 27, 1773.

The *Polly* came up the Delaware late in December, and all unsuspecting, dropped anchor at Chester, twelve miles below Philadelphia. There, one of the handbills was served on Captain Ayres, and he quickly decided to proceed no farther. He was doubtless as little desirous of a personal encounter with the committee who sponsored it as he was of having his cargo burned or tossed into the river.

Now it was precisely at this stage of colonial affairs, when sedition was in the air, that Betsy Griscom took it into her head to toss overboard finally and completely the ties which bound her to Quaker tradition. Possibly the talk she heard everywhere against established institutions put her in the mood. Doubtless the fact that she had just turned twenty-one had much to do with it. At any rate, in defiance of her parents and the Bank Meeting, and while the city was at white heat over the tea tax, she gave her hand in marriage to the Episcopalian, John Ross.

And, furthermore, the young couple did the only thing that seemed to them possible under the circumstances—they slipped quietly out of the city one day, and returned as man and wife.

Not far down the river, on the opposite shore, was the ancient town of Gloucester, in the province of New Jersey—a convenient place, and romantic enough, for just such an adventure. Thither their fancy led them. A tiny but picturesque village, founded over a century before, it nestled in the woods where the Big Timber Creek flowed into the Delaware, a few miles south of Cooper's Ferry, where now stands the city of Camden.

On the very edge of the river in Gloucester Town stood an inn of substantial brick construction, while half a mile back, in a thick clump of walnut trees and magnolias, was a chalybeate spring, famous for its beneficial waters. Hugg's Tavern and the bubbling iron spring made the spot a favorite one for summer jaunts by stage-coach, sailboat or horse ferry. And so hospitable was the inn, with its great brick fireplaces, and so primeval the country roundabout, that the tavern, in other seasons, was the rendezvous of the Gloucester County Fox Hunting Club, organized some years before by gentlemen of Philadelphia.

Perhaps a bit of verse published in Philadelphia in 1772, extolling the sylvan beauties of Gloucester, turned the thoughts of John and Betsy there.

> Sequestered from the city's noise,
>   Its tumults and fantastic joys,
> Fair nymphs and swains retire,
>   Where Delaware's far rolling tide,
> Majestic winds by Glo'ster's side,
>   Whose shades new joys inspire.

Thus ran the opening lines of the poem, penned by the Rev. Nathaniel Evans, of Haddonfield, New

Jersey. But very likely it was a more practical reason than this that drew the eloping pair over "Delaware's rolling tide," judging from the documentary record of their wedding that has come down to us. This record makes it apparent that William Hugg, Jr., the youthful owner of Hugg's Tavern, was a close friend of John Ross, for he it was who went on the bond of the young upholsterer, thus making the ceremony possible.

The laws of the colonies were strict against clandestine marriages. Even where couples professed to be twenty-one, New Jersey required that a bond of 500 pounds sterling be deposited with the officiating clergyman or justice, to guard against the "inticing and deluding of Young Persons" into matrimony. Pennsylvania also required a bond, but not so large in amount.

In the fireproof vaults at Trenton, now capital of New Jersey, filed among colonial records, is the original marriage bond of John Ross and Elizabeth Griscom. Dated November 4, 1773, it bears John's signature and William Hugg's together with that of the justice of the peace, James Bowman, who performed the ceremony.

The Hugg family was an old and prominent one

in Gloucester county. In the stirring days of the Revolution, it was to give generously of its young men to Washington's army, while Hugg's Tavern, which had come into William Hugg's possession from his father, became a rallying point for New Jersey militia. The name of James Bowman, justice of the peace, also appears frequently in the court records of Old Gloucester.

From the marriage bond at Trenton, we have a clear picture of the chain of events that November day so long ago. The river trip by the horse ferry; the visit to Squire Bowman for the marriage license and bond and the simple ceremony which made the eloping couple man and wife; then, as likely as not, supper before one of the great open fires at the inn as the guests of their best man and bondsman; soon followed by the homeward journey.

What excited thoughts were theirs that evening as they traversed the black waters of the river toward the dimly lighted city and the home of Betsy's parents, to which she must return until such time as it proved best to reveal their secret!

Not until the spring of 1774, when their house-keeping plans were completed, did it become known. That the disclosure caused a sensation

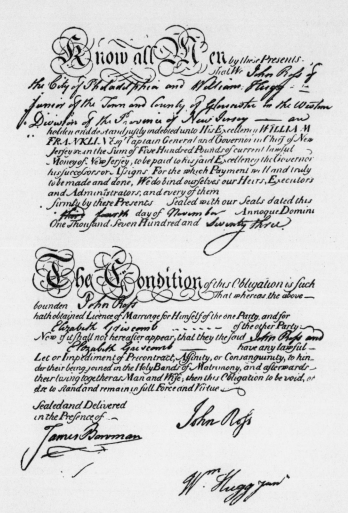

MARRIAGE BOND OF JOHN ROSS AND ELIZABETH GRISCOM (BETSY ROSS)
DATED NOVEMBER 4, 1773. ITS EXISTENCE AND THE DATE AND PLACE
OF THEIR ELOPEMENT REMAINED UNKNOWN UNTIL 1933, WHEN THE
DOCUMENT WAS FOUND AMONG OLD RECORDS AT TRENTON, NEW JERSEY.
AT THE TIME THE FIRST EDITION OF THIS BOOK WAS PUBLISHED IN
1930, THE CIRCUMSTANCES WERE STILL A MYSTERY. WILLIAM FRANKLIN,
NAMED IN THE BOND, WAS THE SON OF BENJAMIN FRANKLIN.

can be inferred from what happened once the Bank Meeting learned that Betsy Griscom was actually the bride of a man outside the faith.   The pre-Revolutionary records of the Society of Friends, painstakingly complete on most subjects that came before it, did not gloss over her transgression.

Let us refer to the minute books of the Philadelphia Monthly Meeting, Northern District, of the year 1774.   Under date of Fourth Month (April) 26, we read that

> *a committee of Women Friends has treated with Elizabeth Rofs, late Grifcom, on account of her marriage with a perfon of another religious perfuafion contrary to the advice of her parents and the good order ufed among us, and fhe does not appear inclined to repent or condemn her breach of duty.*

Thereupon Thomas Scattergood, an elder known for his judgment and piety, was appointed to assist the Women Friends in preparing a Testimony against the young lady, to be read to the Meeting the twenty-fourth of the following month.

In this manner, the wheels of excommunication were set in motion.   Betsy had again been visited, apparently, had been given a chance to repent, even though already married, and had refused. Therefore the committee set about the framing of its indictment, while the Friends of the district awaited the next Monthly Meeting with the affair of Samuel Griscom's daughter much on their minds.

A marked figure she must have been during this interval as she went her ways through the streets, and a frequent subject for talk over cups of tea and in market house gossip. Of all the offenses against the Society which merited expulsion, there were few more serious than marrying out of Meeting, and there was no more solemn or painful occasion in Quaker procedure of colonial days than a session to act on disownment. Few who were accused cared to face the ordeal in person.

The Old Bank Meeting House, where the Monthly Meetings of the Northern District (north of High Street) were at that time held, has long since disappeared in the forward march of the city. It was a square brick building, without trace of ornament, overlooking the Delaware. Set well above the street level, it was reached by two short flights of steps leading through gateways in the brick wall inclosing the meetinghouse yard. The interior, with whitewashed walls, followed the severe style of all Friends' places of worship. On either side of a broad aisle which ran from the door to the farther wall, were ranged the bare, unpainted benches. To the left sat the women and to the right, the men. Facing them was the "gallery," consisting of three rows of high-backed benches, slightly elevated and occupied by the ministers and elders. The business meetings, such as that which considered the case of Betsy Ross, were held on weekdays, either Wednesday or Thursday.

Through the wide doorway entered Friends from all quarters of the Northern District. They included many who were high in the government of the colony—impressive in appearance and bearing. The men were dressed in brown or in full suits of drab, with straight collars and knee breeches. Those of mature years wore broad-brimmed low beaver hats, some of prodigious size, which they kept on their heads during meeting, sitting with hands crossed on the tops of their canes. A few of the well to do had silver buckles on their shoes and at their knees, and their canes were gold-headed.

The women elders wore gowns of gray, with white silken kerchiefs folded in front, and black "sugar scoop" bonnets of silk. When moved to exhortation, they would remove their bonnets, perhaps hanging them on the end of the gallery rail in front, and, when finished, replace them before taking their seats.

Always a meeting for worship came first—a long period of silence broken only by those inspired by the "inner light" to speak or lead in prayer. At its close, a voice from the gallery announced, "The shutters will now be lowered." Whereupon a movable partition was let down in sections from the ceiling, separating the men and the women completely for the business sessions.

In an atmosphere tense with expectation, that May morning in 1774, each meeting awaited the important business of the day—the Testimony prepared by Thomas Scattergood's committee against Elizabeth Ross. By a strange coincidence, that same year, Hannah Cathrall, as presiding clerk, was the leader of the women's meetings and directed the proceedings. She it was who, years before, had taught Betsy Griscom her A, B, C's at Rebecca Jones's School in Drinker's

Alley. With what mingled feelings now she sat in judgment over her former pupil! And at the head of the men's meeting, was Henry Drinker, of the firm of James and Drinker!

Whether Samuel and Rebecca Griscom braved their humiliation enough to be present, or others of her family, we do not know. Usually at such proceedings there were many remarks, and prayers for the straying Friend, trying indeed to those near of kin. The yellowed pages of the old minute book give us our only record of the session as follows:

> *24th 5th Mo. 1774.*
>
> *A Teſtimony having been prepared as directed laſt month in the caſe of Elizabeth Roſs, John Parriſh and John Thomſon in company with ſuch Women Friends as may be appointed at their Meeting, are deſired to deliver to her a copy of ſaid Teſtimony and acquaint her with her right of appealing, it being as follows:*
>
> *Elizabeth Roſs, late Griſcom of the Northern Diſtrict of this City, having had her education and made profeſſion with us, the people called Quakers, but for want of taking heed to the dictates of Truth in her mind, hath ſo far deviated therefrom as to be married to a man of another religious perſuaſion— without conſent of her parents,—for which diſorderly and undutiful conduct ſhe hath been treated with,*

But our labors of love not having the defired effect,
we hereby teftify that fhe hath difunited herfelf from
Religious Fellowfhip with us, until through Repent-
ance and amendment of Life, fhe feeks to make
fuch acknowledgment to this Meeting as the nature
of her cafe requires, which we defire fhe may be en-
abled to do through the affiftance of Divine Grace.

The accused young woman apparently did not
choose to be present and hear the discussion. She
could have attended and made a statement in her
own behalf had she wished, but judging from the
records, she preferred to ignore the whole matter.

Soon afterward, however, the joint committee,
headed by John Parrish and Hannah Cathrall,
carried out its instructions and once more a visit
was made to the little house in Arch Street where
John and Betsy Ross had taken up their abode.
More than ordinary efforts were used to bring her
to repentance for her "diforderly and undutiful
action," but in vain. At the June Monthly
Meeting, they reported, according to the minutes,
that they had "delivered to Elizabeth Rofs,
late Grifcom, our Teftimony againft her mif-
conduct and that fhe appeared to be fatisfied
with Friends' proceedings in her cafe." Thomas

5

Scattergood was thereupon instructed to read such Testimony at the close of one of the First-day morning meetings, which he did the very next week.

There was none in the membership of Friends more revered than Thomas Scattergood. Kindly by nature, and known through the city for his charitable acts, he was frequently called upon by the Meeting for responsible duties, often unpleasant, requiring tact and force. On one occasion, a chronicler of the times relates, he and William Savery, also a prominent minister in the Society, had a concern to be present at the execution of two criminals. In those days the hangings were held in public places as examples to evildoers— the most public of all being at Third and High Streets, at the west end of the market house, near the whipping post and pillory.

When they arrived at the platform, the two Friends ascended the ladder after the condemned men. Following the execution, standing beside the swaying bodies, William Savery, the chronicler states, "felt a powerful impreſſion to addreſs the multitude aſſembled. Thomas Scattergood followed and very impreſſively and powerfully pointed

out to the people the evil of giving way to the firſt
temptation to do wrong, cloſing the whole with
ſupplication. Many of the ſpectators wept during
the diſcourſes."

During the months in which the Monthly
Meeting was laboring with Elizabeth Ross, it may
be taken for granted that Thomas Scattergood
handled the case with all the forbearance possible,
yet with the firmness which its gravity demanded.

VI

War Clouds

THE house to which John Ross had taken his bride, and which is now a national land-mark, was one of those small, narrow, brick struc-tures with sharply sloping roofs which lined virtually all the streets of colonial Philadelphia. In the old quarter of the city you can see many of them still, with buildings of later periods towering beside them.

It was a two-and-a-half-story dwelling at 89 Arch Street (later numbered 239) which they leased as their abode. Like most of its neighbors, it had a little shop in front. This John and Betsy found admirably suited to the upholstery business, in which they immediately engaged. Neither dis-ownment by the Society of Friends nor the annoy-ing tactics of King George of England weighed seriously upon them during those first months of their honeymoon. The war talk was waxing hotter, to be sure, but few in Philadelphia believed that the colonies would actually come to grips with their rulers across the sea.

John Ross, skilled at his trade, plunged vigorously into the fascinating task of building up a business for himself. His wife divided her time between housekeeping and helping him, and life indeed had a rosy outlook. All through the neighborhood were like scenes of industry and thrift, which, duplicated through the land, were laying the foundations of America's greatness. In Arch Street and the cross streets, busy shops with their swinging signs, energetically bidding for trade. Apothecary shops and stove and crockery shops, blacksmiths and whitesmiths, snuff shops and coppersmiths, ironmongers and the very necessary stores selling groceries and dry goods.

Philadelphia was at that time hardly more than a large village, with landscapes of rolling country spreading widely to the north, west, and south, dotted with white farmhouses and crossroads hamlets. The City of Penn, then the metropolis of the new world, had approximately 20,000 inhabitants and all lived within the sound of the State House bell. There were few frame houses. Practically all were of brick within the town, two stories or three stories in height, and were used for both residence and business purposes. The foremost merchants lived and carried on their trade in Front Street and Water Street overlooking the Delaware —their wives and daughters assisting in the shops.

Travel was infrequent except by the privileged. The mails were few. The stagecoach, the tallow candle, and the spinning wheel largely regulated the affairs of men. Until Doctor Franklin brought out his wonderful contraption, the Franklin stove, all heating and cooking depended upon the open fireplace with its swinging row of pots and kettles. At a cost of twenty shillings, a traveler could be transported with his baggage to New York, and hope to reach there in two days, providing everything went well and the wheels sank not too deeply into quagmires and snow banks.

After dark, the streets were dimly lighted by sputtering whale-oil lamps on wooden posts at the corners. As dusk fell, watchmen were seen here and there trimming and lighting the lamps—and through the quiet stretches of the night, their voices were heard loudly crying the hours.

William Penn, in laying out the city, had encouraged the building of detached houses with rustic porches and trailing plants and shade trees, for he wished Philadelphia to be a "greene coun-

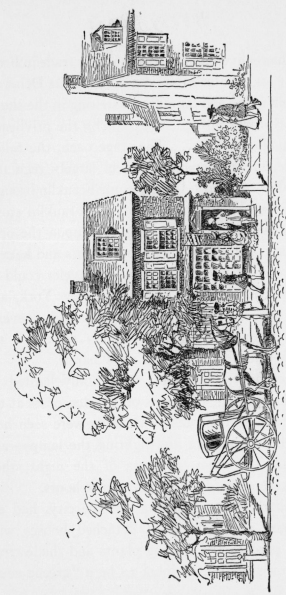

Trade Was Brisk at the Upholstery Shop of John and Betsy Ross.

try town° which might never be burnt and might always be wholefome." The entire city, with its houses, squares, and gardens, as he planned it, was to cover twelve square miles. Two streets, High and Broad, were to be one hundred feet wide and were to intersect, with a large open space at the place they crossed, to be called Centre Square. Eight streets, each fifty feet wide, were to be laid out parallel to High Street, and twenty of the same width parallel to the Delaware, in checker-board style.

John Ross found his bride an apt helpmate at the upholstering art, and their business was brisk from the start. Betsy was artistic and engaging. Constantly their little shop was filled with chairs done in plain horsehair, couches of worsted dam-ask, and carved mahogany or red-walnut bed-steads—all undergoing construction or perhaps refinishing for well-to-do patrons. Frequently standing before their door were seen the popular two-wheeled chaises and sometimes paneled car-riages which had brought their owners on visits of inspection or purchase.

Sunday mornings found the young couple at worship at Christ Church in Second Street, just around the corner from their home, Betsy having readily agreed to that arrangement, strange though the forms were to the girl brought up so strictly in the Quaker faith.

Christ Church, with its tall steeple, had been a familiar sight to her from her earliest recollections, as indeed to the oldest inhabitant. As a child, walking to the silent Meeting House on the river bank with the plain-garbed Friends, she had marveled at the very different procession turning into Second Street. For the Sabbath there brought a peal of bells and the rustle of silks and a parade of finery which had given her a glimpse of a new and strange world. The men, in their ruffled shirts, their purple coats and waist-coats, their freshly powdered wigs and three-cornered hats, were not the least of her astonishments. Little did she dream then that one day she would be a part of that fashionable Episcopal promenade.

Ever since 1695, the followers of the Church of England had worshiped at Christ Church— first in a smaller edifice and then in the classic brick structure erected in 1727. Here went the colonial governors, not of the Quaker faith, and other officers of state with their families. Here walked the venerable Doctor Franklin from his home, at that time at Second and Race Streets; and here later went Washington and Adams and Jefferson with their households. Here also worshiped the members of the Continental Congress during the critical days soon to come.

Christ Church stands today unchanged since Revolutionary times, and just under the high pulpit, with its spiral stairway, is pew number 12,

THEY WORSHIPED AT CHRIST CHURCH, THE "PATRIOTS' SANCTUARY"

in which John and Betsy Ross sat and worshiped during their brief period of happiness together. The pew is small, seating but two persons, and is separated by a column rising to the lofty ceiling from the one later occupied by General and Lady Washington. It is marked by an American flag with thirteen stars and by a bronze plate bearing the following inscription:

Here worshipped

MRS. ELIZABETH ROSS

who, under the direction

of a Committee of

Continental Congress

composed of

GEORGE WASHINGTON

ROBERT MORRIS

and

GEORGE ROSS

was the maker of the

FIRST AMERICAN FLAG

* * * * *

And so, engrossed with their shopkeeping and their churchgoing, and living very much to themselves, John and Betsy passed that first blissful spring of their married career. It was not a case of all work and no play by any means. Sunday, a day of worship, was also a day of harmless diversion—of calls upon intimate friends; of happy afternoon rambles into the country or occasionally a drive for longer distances in a chaise hired from some near-by liveryman.

Out Second Street was a favorite drive in blossom time for Philadelphians. Just beyond the point at which a giant suspension bridge now spans the Delaware, the houses were few and the street became a rutted road of clay, which, at the famous Bull's Head Tavern, forked to the left into the Germantown Turnpike. Now a congested city street, this highway at that time wound through rich farm and orchard land and patches of woods, with a gentle ascent all the way to Chestnut Hill. The right fork continued as the old Second Street Pike, from which branched the much traveled Frankford Road. Following the course of the river, it was the preferred stage route to Frankford, Bristol, and New York.

It was down that stage route that much of the news of the outside world came—particularly from the northern colonies, and it was down that road that alarming reports now traveled as the spring of '74 advanced into summer. Reports which shook the city to its foundations put an end to honeymoon tranquillity in the home of John Ross, and drove from everybody's head all topics save the one most dreaded—WAR!

Apparently nothing could now stop it or long postpone it. Massachusetts, it was declared, was in open revolt. Parliament, angered by the Boston Tea Party, had closed the port of Boston. More citizens had been shot down in the streets by British soldiery. Paul Revere, an able and vigorous young patriot, was on his way to Pennsylvania as an emissary to urge the calling of a congress of all the colonies.

Philadelphians heard of secret meetings at the homes of the city's leaders. Despatch riders were seen coming and going. Loyalists, in counter meetings, issued pamphlets denouncing all traitors to the king. A Committee of Safety was organized by Doctor Franklin to decide what Pennsylvania should do.

Then one fall day there came a sudden request to the Carpenters' Company that they turn over their hall, a fine brick building facing Chestnut Street, for the purpose of a meeting of the first Continental Congress.

Samuel Griscom and his carpenter associates were astounded.

"Why their building?" they asked.

The State House was occupied by the Pennsylvania provincial assembly then in session, they were told, and Pennsylvania was under a royal governor! Carpenters' Hall, with its large assembly room and substantial appearance, was the next logical place. Delegates were even then hurrying to Philadelphia from all the colonies; arrangements must be made and made quickly. The lives and liberty of the people depended on action.

Still some of the carpenters hesitated. Their time-honored society, modeled after the guilds of England, had always been loyal to the king. Patriotism clashed with loyalty.

British officers living in Philadelphia freely predicted they would never dare give their consent to such treasonable purposes. A royalist newspaper published a warning that should they do so, "their necks might be inconveniently lengthened."

But these threats only spurred the carpenters to decision. They called a meeting of all their members to consider the subject; and once assembled, they quickly acted. Their old minute book bears this record:

On the queſtion being put, "ſhall they be allowed to meet here," voted that they ſhall.

From then on events moved swiftly. What happened is known to every American schoolboy. The meeting of the Congress; the impassioned speeches of Patrick Henry and Samuel Adams; the petition to George III giving him one last chance to mend his ways. Then, in April, 1775, the startling news of Lexington Green and Concord Bridge, which fanned the smoldering fires of revolt into a mighty blaze from Massachusetts to South Carolina.

At a second Congress, assembled in the State House, from which the legislature and the royal governor were ousted, it was declared that war was now an actual fact. The time for petitioning was past. John Hancock of Massachusetts presided. Leading the debate were such men as Franklin, Robert Morris, and George Ross, of

Pennsylvania; Francis Hopkinson and William
Livingston, of New Jersey; Samuel and John
Adams, of Massachusetts; Richard Henry Lee
and Patrick Henry, of Virginia. They were of
one mind, and decisions came quickly.

It was resolved to appoint a Council of Twelve
to have full executive power. It was voted to
appoint George Washington of Virginia, whose
military talents and experience they all recognized,
commander in chief of all the armed forces of the
Colonies. It was voted that he proceed as quickly
as possible to Massachusetts and take command of
the army encamped before Boston, which had
now been seized by British regiments.

Philadelphia, the quiet Quaker city, thus became, to the astonishment of its citizens, the
pivotal point of this whole vast disturbance.
Betsy Ross and her husband, like hundreds of
their fellow townsmen, viewed with bewilderment
the rush of events which suddenly turned their
city into a revolutionary capital.

On the morning of the twenty-first of June, they
learned that Washington was that afternoon setting out for Boston. So, sharing the public curi-
osity to see the new commander, they hastened to

the State House, to which, it seemed, everyone else in the city had repaired. Wealthy Tories rubbed elbows with the king's rebellious subjects, and stood silent and disdainful in the cheering throng as the stalwart Virginian leaped into his saddle and rode briskly down Chestnut Street, escorted by a company of the Philadelphia Light Horse.

Thus did the colonists launch their stupendous, and as so many thousands thought, their fool-hardy and wicked effort to combat the mighty power of Great Britain. Their appointed leader had before him one of the greatest tasks that was ever allotted to man to undertake. In long, wasting campaigns, through bitter years of misfortune, discouragement, and bloodshed, he was to carry the fight before victory finally crowned his work and brilliantly justified the trust placed in him.

Doubtless few thoughts of such contingencies were in the mind of Washington or the minds of those who watched him as he departed that June afternoon on his mission. And certainly the wife of John Ross, upholsterer, had no inkling of the part she was to play in the national drama when next he returned to Philadelphia.

"He was now in the vigor of his days," states an early nineteenth century biographer of the Father of his Country—"forty-three years of age, stately in appearance, noble in his demeanor, calm and dignified in his deportment. As he sat his horse with manly grace, his military presence delighted every eye."

VII

The First Sacrifice

PHILADELPHIA was now in a seethe of war
preparations. Congress remained in continuous session. Measures designed to give the
commander in chief full support were passed
quickly and with but little debate, and express
riders spurred their horses to the north and
south with dispatches to the provincial capitals
telling what was expected of them in men and
money.

Through High Street and Chestnut Street in
the warm June weather, the roll of drums and the
shrill song of the fife told of marching militia.
The open lots bordering the governor's woods
sprang into sudden usefulness as parade grounds.

Warlike displays of swords, pistols, muskets,
and knapsacks monopolized the windows of hardware shops, while here and there the Pine Tree
flag of New England and Rattlesnake flags, with
their admonition "Don't Tread on Me," waved
in competition with the Union Jack.

The alignment of Tories and Whigs took shape rapidly. The Tory party was strong in Philadelphia. For here the wealthy, leisured, social leadership class, especially among the Episcopalians, was a larger group than in other cities— rich merchants and importers who dreaded the interruption of trade, being outspoken in their allegiance to the crown.

The streets around the State House were thronged with excited men in loud, angry argument. Feeling was particularly bitter toward a third group—the Quakers. As a body, they actively sided with neither party. True to the teachings of George Fox and William Penn, they strictly forbade any member to take up arms either for England or America. But many a young man of "thee" and "thou" speech nevertheless discarded his broad-brimmed hat to shoulder a gun or buckle on a sword to join the militia—and was disowned by the Friends for doing so. The disownment, of course, was just as prompt if he, perchance, went over to the forces of the king.

Enlistment went on rapidly. All classes responded. Young men with military experience were encouraged to form companies of their own, and in the absence of a standard uniform, strange and fantastic garbs appeared. "Captain Thomas Forrest," according to one writer, "dressed his men in the style of Indians, with painted faces, leggings, and plumes. Captain Cowperthwaite organized a company of young Quakers called the 'Quaker Blues.' Captain John Cadwalader formed a company of 'Greens,' called, in allusion to the gentility of the members, 'the silk stocking company.'"

Recruiting stations established at the public houses brought good business to the proprietors. The large new City Tavern in south Second Street, the famous Indian Queen at the southeast corner of Fourth and High Streets, and the Cross Keys Tavern in Chestnut at Third Street, were crowded day and night by idlers, who, as they drank their ale, were harangued by soldier orators who pilloried the tyrant king and those daring to support him. Many a blow was struck as muddled patrons resented aspersions on their political beliefs.

Business was especially brisk with the genial John Nicholson, who conducted the Indian Queen. For this old hostelry, directly opposite the royal post office, had long been the headquarters and destination of the stage lines and now became a center of war news and gossip. News from the North was awaited with breathless interest—and the arrival of the New York post brought people on the run. Each morning, as the swaying coach rumbled up High Street and turned into the cobblestone stableyard, the great room of the inn would be emptied as if by magic, and the driver and his passengers were often hard put to avoid rough handling as the crowd beset them for tidings. Any item from the Boston district, true or false, flew on wings about the city.

Arch Street and its community of Friends were sadly shaken by these feverish events. From her position outside the Society, Betsy Ross, with

THE ARRIVAL OF THE NEW YORK POST BROUGHT PEOPLE ON THE RUN

mingled feelings, saw disagreements in the ranks
of prominent members compared with which the
defections due to marriage had been small indeed.
She saw such Quaker families as the Morrises, the
Logans, the Mifflins, and the Biddles, socially and
politically important, openly siding with the
American cause, and leaving the Society of Friends.
She saw others, equally prominent, like the Pem-
bertons, the Shippens, and the Walns, going quietly
on with their religious and business pursuits and
either refusing to take any part in the war or
through a traditional sense of loyalty, leaning
toward the British side.

As to her own husband, Betsy knew exactly
what would happen on the enlistment question,
and it soon came to pass. John Ross, saying
little and thinking much, cast his lot with the
patriot cause. He came of a family used to active
participation in public affairs and the thought of
remaining aloof from this great adventure probably did not enter his head.

An uncle, George Ross, was a member of the
Continental Congress and an active leader in the
war councils. Another uncle, John Ross, was an
eloquent lawyer, a vestryman of Christ Church,

and for some time had held the high position of
Royal Attorney General for the colony. The Ross
family, however, was a conspicuous example of a
divided house, for John, the Attorney General,
disagreeing with his brothers, was decidedly of
Tory sympathies. He considered it his duty to
retain allegiance to his sovereign and, like the
Quakers, to endeavor to reconcile the two
countries.

It was not in Betsy Ross's make-up to oppose
in any way her young husband's decision to enlist.
In the gathering storm, she adopted his views and
feelings and pledged herself to the fortunes of a
soldier's wife. She could not foresee that in a few
short months, those fortunes would take him from
her. But even had she been able to penetrate
the future, it is doubtful that her attitude would
have been different. She was of the group of
"fighting Quakers," whose burning zeal for the
cause comes down to us as a vivid picture against
the war's tragic background. Later on, as the
conflict was drawing to a close, she helped to
organize that group into a separate religious
society which endured for many years after peace
was signed.

In those stirring days of 1775, the securing of
military supplies was a grave problem. There
was a sad dearth of them in the colonies, and a
secret committee was appointed by Congress to
procure ammunition and guns for Washington's
army. Small quantities were soon brought from
the West Indies by brave ship captains who defied
capture by the British, and stored at various ports.

It fell to Esek Hopkins, commodore of an em-
bryo American navy, however, to supply the
army's immediate needs in impressive fashion.
Congress had fitted out with guns a fleet of seven
merchantmen in the Delaware, as the initial step
toward presenting some opposition to King
George's fine frigates, and Hopkins, a skilled and
daring skipper from Rhode Island, was appointed
early in December to command the squadron.

Selecting the *Alfred*, formerly a merchantman
called the *Black Prince*, as his flagship, he sailed
boldly out of the river, looking for British warships or privateers. Meeting none, he shaped
his course for the Bahama Islands belonging to
Great Britain. He knew that at New Providence,
capital of the Bahamas, was a large store of just
what the colonies needed most.

The governor of the islands, taken completely by surprise, made but feeble resistance. That the rebels possessed a fleet and such a degree of audacity was farthest from his thoughts. Hopkins' sailors and marines stormed the fort at night and carried off all the powder, shot, and guns they could find, and Governor Brown besides. More than a hundred shining brass cannon were captured in the raid.

When the little squadron sailed up the Delaware again, it received a riotous welcome. Staid Philadelphia, beside itself with excitement, proclaimed Hopkins the hero of the hour—and the exploits of his infant navy, heralded far and wide, gave the colonies their first real thrill of sea power.

The munitions thus provided by bold skippers, however, which took such a weight off the minds of the anxious leaders at the State House, by a cruel twist of fate brought tragedy to the home of a young patriot who lived in Arch Street.

For six months, John Ross had served in the Pennsylvania militia, faithfully drilling with his company, helping now and then in the recruiting service, and awaiting the time when he might be ordered to the front. Now, with the arrival of precious stores of munitions, he was assigned new duties. Quantities of these supplies, as quickly as they were unloaded, were hurried northward to Washington's troops, while the remainder was stored in rough buildings on the wharves in the southern part of the city, under strong guard of young men of the militia. To this work, John Ross was detailed.

A rather commonplace and undramatic duty it probably seemed to him and not at all what he would have wished for in an active path to glory, but it had one redeeming feature—he could still manage to be at home at frequent intervals. And doubtless it was a matter of rejoicing on Betsy's part that his duties were keeping him so near her instead of sending him to far-off Boston and the perils attending Washington's siege.

She now took upon her capable shoulders the full charge of their little shop. The game of business had engrossed her and the increased responsibility only added to the zest. She hummed happily to herself as she stitched the coverings for chairs and sofas, glanced out at the wintry street with its leafless rows of linden trees and heard the distant rattle of drums with but little foreboding.

The war would soon be a thing of the past; everybody said so; her husband would cast aside his uniform; trade would come more and more their way and, who knows, perhaps she might soon be sewing on clothes for some tiny person whose arrival would fill their cup of joy to overflowing.

Pathetic optimism! She was living in a false paradise, from which, as in the cases of so many wives and mothers throughout that harassed land, there was to be a rude awakening.

There came an afternoon late in January. Its events and its anguish were seared in her memory.

Most of the day it had been snowing—a heavy wet snow blown in by an east wind off the river, and turning to sleet as night came on. Arch Street lay deep in slush. Just before dusk, a detail of men in the uniform of the Pennsylvania militia stopped before the house at Number 89. One of them rapped on the door. He was a friend of the occupants and had been on that account selected as spokesman. Betsy, answering, began a cheery greeting, but something in his face stopped her short.

There had been an accident, he told her with halting speech—an explosion of gunpowder on the wharf. Wide-eyed she looked at him, incredulous. Fear suddenly reached down into her heart—fear which instantly rose to sickening terror, numbed her brain, and made her clutch the doorway for support—for beyond him in the street, their uniforms grayed by the falling sleet, she saw a group carrying toward her the broken, bleeding, and unconscious form of the one she loved most on earth.

Thus the happiness which this young woman had gone through so much to secure, was in the twinkling of an eye wrested from her. Alienated from her family and her faith, dazed by the sudden collapse of all her dreams, she wept while death stalked into her little bedroom. It was the first great sacrifice she was called upon to make in liberty's cause.

VIII

War's Anxieties

THE bells in the steeple of Christ Church tolled softly as a little funeral procession slowly made its way along the ice-coated sidewalk to the cemetery at Fifth and Arch Streets. There, John Ross, the first member of the parish to give up his life in the struggle for independence, was laid to rest. Like hundreds of soldiers and sailors who soon followed him behind those brick walls, he sleeps in an unidentified grave, many of the headstones long since having crumbled away.

In the Revolutionary records of Christ Church, we find this simple notation, "John Rofs, upholſterer, died January 21, 1776. Buried in C. C." (Christ Church Burial Ground). Page after page of deaths then follow, similarly brief, nothing given of the circumstances—simply the names, dates, and places of interment—eloquent enough testimony of war's grim harvest.

After that trying day when she saw her husband's body lowered into the snow-covered ground,

Elizabeth Ross turned a brave countenance to the world, and busied herself with might and main in the duties of her home and shop. She was young, just past her twenty-fourth birthday, and in that fact, together with her buoyant nature, lay her ability to lift herself from her weight of sorrow.

On Sundays, she sought comfort in the services at the old church to which her husband had been so devoted and, as the war went on, her spare moments from business found her occupied like women all about her in the making of sorely needed garments for the army. Her initiative and skill soon made her a neighborhood leader in this important work.

Sunday worship brought her into frequent contact with prominent members of Christ Church and widened her acquaintance. It also kept her in touch with important developments. Many delegates to the Continental Congress had pews there, notably George Ross, who never failed to give a kindly word of greeting to his nephew's widow or to inquire as to her welfare. Occasionally on week days too, the delegates were seen at devotion at the church. It was their custom in the first years of the war to go there in a body for special prayers conducted by the rector. From the State House at Sixth and Chestnut Streets, it was but a few minutes' walk to the "Patriots' Sanctuary."

Betsy charmed Colonel Ross as she charmed all men, and he was both amused and interested by her ardor for the patriot cause. Her witty sallies at the expense of King George and his policies brought many a laugh from the dignified statesmen as they stood in groups about the brick-paved yard following the Rev. Duche's sermons. Of those men who guided the destinies of the young nation, many, including Colonel Ross, Benjamin Franklin, and five other signers of the Declaration of Independence, now lie buried beside the church or in the walled cemetery three squares away.

During these days of her early widowhood, it happened also that Betsy was thrown much with the parents and sisters of her old flame, John Claypoole, who were devoted members of Christ Church. Susannah, Martha, and Clarissa Sidney Claypoole, old school friends, made her constantly welcome at their home in Fourth Street. John, their only brother, away on militia duty, they

seldom saw—but their talk was full enough of
him, and Betsy followed with interest each bit of
news about her former wooer.

The Claypoole tannery and family fortunes had
suffered much since the king had declared his
American subjects in a state of rebellion. Bun-
dles of hides were no longer trundled into ships
and sent over seas. War furnished the principal
food for conversation—war and John's prospects
in it.

There was another topic, however, which that
young man's father was fond of bringing up when
in a jesting mood and Betsy sat at the family
board. He, William Claypoole, boasting a long
line of Quaker ancestry, had been "read out of
Meeting" years before for wedding Elizabeth
Hall, daughter of John Hall, mariner, of the
Episcopal faith. To twit Betsy about the error
of her ways which had caused her eviction from
the Bank Meeting, therefore seemed to be his
particular amusement. He never lost an opportunity of referring to it. And if his motive was to
stir their pretty guest to some spirited comment
on his own transgression, he never failed to do
that either.

7

As the winter melted into spring and crocuses and daffodils dotted the side yards in Arch Street, the whole country became more and more absorbed in the great conflict. With the breaking up of the cold weather, the struggle had taken on real activity. General Sir William Howe had evacuated Boston after an all-winter siege by Washington's Continental troops, and had set sail for New York in the British fleet. Sir Henry Clinton, with a large force, had gone on to South Carolina to attack the southern provinces, while General Howe and Lord Cornwallis turned their attention to New York.

Washington, who had previously dispatched General Charles Lee southward to keep his eye on Howe, soon followed with his main army, arriving at New York the middle of April. Fortune had not favored him. With his ill-trained, badly clothed troops and dwindling military supplies, he had conducted, it is true, a masterly siege of a far superior force in Boston, but the British threat against New York and the south now made the outlook black indeed. To add to his burdens, there were serious reverses in Canada. General Montgomery's expedition to Quebec, of which so much had been expected, had ended in flat failure.

In May, upon learning of this, Washington sent General Horatio Gates to Philadelphia to lay the Canadian dispatches before Congress. But scarcely had Gates arrived and revealed his bad news when Congress decided to talk the situation over with the commander in chief himself and summoned him from New York to discuss the coming campaign.

John Hancock, president of the Congress, thereupon took this occasion to invite General and Mrs. Washington to be his guests at his Arch Street residence while in Philadelphia. It was the first time the American commander had been in the capital since he had hurried away to New England the preceding summer. Mrs. Washington had traveled from her home in Mount Vernon in the fall to join her husband in his camp before Boston, and her comfort was apparently much on the mind of the courteous Hancock as he wrote:

> . . . *I hope the fituation of the great affairs with which you are intrufted will admit your making this excurfion which I apprehend may be ferviceable to*

your health, in which cafe I requeſt that you will pleaſe to honor me with your and your Lady's company at my Houſe, where I have a Bed at your ſervice during your continuance here, and where every endeavor of mine and Mrs. Hancock ſhall be extended to make your abode agreeable.

I reſide in an airy open part of the City, in Arch ſtreet and Fourth ſtreet. If this ſhould be agreeable to you it will give me much pleaſure.

I am to inform you that Congreſs have this day appointed Horatio Gates, Eſq., a Major General, and Thomas Mifflin, Eſq., a Brigadier General in the Continental Army. A commiſſion for the former I tranſmit by this opportunity. I have delivered one to Mr. Mifflin here.

I have the Honor to be with reſpectful ſentiments and eſteem,

Sir, your moſt obt. hbl. ſert.,

John Hancock, Preſident.

P. S. Since writing the foregoing, I have been told that your Lady, not having had the Small-Pox, has intentions of taking it by Inoculation in this City. I beg that that circumſtance may be no prevention to your making uſe of my Houſe; it is large and very Commodious, and every accommodation about it is at your ſervice, and you may depend that Mrs. Hancock will give the greateſt

attention to your Lady, ſhould ſhe incline to take the Diſorder. I ſhall be peculiarly happy if my invitation may be found agreeable to you.
His Excellency
    General Waſhington.

Washington left General Israel Putnam, the fighting New Englander, in charge of the army at New York, with instructions what to do in case of an enemy attack, and on the twenty-first of May, set out for Philadelphia with Mrs. Washington. Great was the stir in the Quaker City as Lady Washington's "chariot and four, with black postilions in scarlet and white liveries," in which she had traveled from Virginia the year before, rolled up Chestnut Street to the State House, with a company of cavalry acting as escort to her illustrious husband.

The visit of the commander in chief was a timely one for the good of the patriot cause. Congress had moved slowly in furnishing troops and supplies—much too slowly, in his opinion—and apparently failed to realize, far from the battle front, the dire needs of the army. Among some of the members there was hope even yet of conciliation with King George.

"I am extremely glad, dear General," wrote one of Washington's commanders, "that you are in Philadelphia, for their councils sometimes lack a little of military electricity."

"In his conferences with Congress, Washington appears to have furnished this electricity," says a biographer of the Father of His Country.

He told the members that no reconciliation could be made with Great Britain on acceptable terms, and that it was evident the king was determined to fight until there was complete submission by the colonies. A long war was therefore inevitable, but it was impossible to carry it on with the scanty force composing the Continental Army.

As a result of his appeals, Congress immediately passed resolutions, greatly increasing the army at New York, providing fire rafts to prevent the entrance of the enemy fleet into the harbor and establishing a flying camp of ten thousand militia to be stationed in New Jersey for the defense of the middle colonies. Another important measure was the creation of a war office, with military affairs concentrated under a "Board of War and Ordnance," which could act without the delays that had been such a handicap in the past.

"We expect a bloody fummer in New York and Canada," wrote Washington a little later to his brother Auguftine, "and I am forry to fay that we are not, either in men or arms, prepared for it. However, it is to be hoped that, if our caufe is juft, as I moft religioufly believe it, the fame Providence which has in many inftances appeared for us, will ftill go on to afford its aid."

IX

Colonial Flags

IT was during General Washington's visit to
Philadelphia in the spring of 1776 that the
most important event of Betsy Ross's life occurred.
Let us first relate, however, some of the circumstances which brought it about, and which caused
the great leader to seek her assistance.

One of the deficiencies he had keenly felt since
taking command of the Continental forces was the
lack of national colors on land and sea. He had
urged the adoption of a standard flag, and as
events swept on toward complete severance from
Great Britain, the need became more acute. In
Philadelphia, he found Franklin, Hancock, Adams,
and other leaders in Congress, spurred on by the
Virginia delegates, talking Independence as an inevitable fact. He himself realized that it was a
question of only a few days or weeks. Thomas
Paine, Quaker though he was, had argued for it
in blistering pamphlets. On the streets and in the
taverns it was the uppermost topic.

Every military instinct told the commander in chief the need of a standard emblem for the new nation that was about to come into being. From the beginnings of history, he knew that in all their struggles for dominion or against tyranny, men had followed a flag. Savage tribes, in their primitive warfare, had carried aloft on poles skins of animals, painted with crude designs to distinguish them from hostile tribes. The Egyptians had carried the figures of sacred objects at the ends of their spears, and cloth banners bearing a king's name or other identifying device. Early Persian, Greek, and Roman generals had used military standards consisting of symbols fixed at the tops of towers or elevated places—rallying points in battle; the name standard originally coming from their being stationary. Later the Romans carried banners of silk which were guarded with the greatest jealousy by the bravest men of the army. The Knights Templar, formed by nine French knights, followed Godfrey de Bouillon to the crusades, carrying a banner attached by nine rings to a crossbar and reading, "Non nobis, Domine, non nobis, sed nomini tuo da gloriam." (Not to us, Lord, not to us, but to thy name give glory.)

Facing his own tremendous problems, Washington was well aware of the influence of a flag on the mind of every soldier—its stimulus toward patriotism and loyalty, its inspiration in the face of danger, privation, and discouragement. A source of weakness in his forces was the intense dislike and jealousy with which the militia of the different States regarded each other. The Virginians sneered at the New England merchants as "peasants and shopkeepers." The New Englanders sneered back at the "lazy squires." Religious differences and boundary disputes also made trouble. The unifying effect of a national symbol would be of incalculable value. Moreover, there was the prime necessity of a visible sign of this unity of the colonies—an emblem by which their ships and battalions could be quickly distinguished from those of the enemy.

At the start of the Revolution, different colonies or sections had their own colors—and some of these displayed such striking designs and mottoes that they continued in service with modifications through a great part of the war. One was the "Pine Tree Flag" of New England, with the red cross of St. George and a green pine tree in the upper corner. Another was the "Rattlesnake Flag," which appeared in several designs—the most common being a rattlesnake in the center, coiled and ready to strike, and under it the words, "Don't Tread on Me."

A third was the flag designed by Colonel William Moultrie, of South Carolina—a large blue banner with a silver crescent in one corner. New York had a flag showing a black beaver on a white field. Rhode Island's design was a white field with a blue anchor, over which was the word "Hope," and occasionally a cluster of stars in the corner.

In commenting on the flags that were seen waving at the outbreak of the war, one writer said, "They were as various as the troops were motley."

Washington reached the camp at Cambridge to take command of the army early in July, 1775. On October 20, Colonel Joseph Reed, of Philadelphia, his secretary, doubtless at his chief's direction, wrote from Cambridge to two officers, Colonel Glover and Colonel Moylan, "Pleaſe fix upon ſome particular color for a flag, and a ſignal by which our veſſels may know one another. What do you think of a flag with a white ground, and a tree in the middle—the motto 'An appeal to

Heaven.' This is the flag of our floating batteries."
The suggested modification of the Pine Tree Flag
was acted on and had considerable use, especially
on the sea.

Shortly after the date of Colonel Reed's letter,
a committee from Congress visited Washington at
Cambridge. It consisted of Benjamin Franklin,
Thomas Lynch, and Benjamin Harrison, and
according to the resolution appointing them, they
were to confer with the commander in chief and
with the governors of adjacent colonies, "touching
the most effectual method of continuing, supporting
and regulating a Continental Army."

Of the many subjects discussed with Washington, one is believed to have been a standard banner,
for on January 2, 1776, the "Grand Union" or
"Cambridge" Flag, of entirely new design, was
hoisted over the camp before Boston. It consisted of thirteen stripes with the British Union
Jack in the corner. For a hundred fifty years
the colonies had been faithful to the mother country. The retention of the king's colors or union
jack with its blended crosses of St. George and
St. Andrew, represented the still recognized sover-
eignty of England, and the alternate red and white

stripes symbolized the union of the thirteen colonies against her tyranny and oppression.

The idea of stripes was not new to flags and frequently occurred in heraldic designs. The coat of arms of the Washington family, for example, contained three five-pointed stars and two red stripes. This prompted Rear Admiral George H. Preble, U. S. N., in his book entitled *Our Flag*, to say, "Without wandering far, seeking the origin of the stripes upon our flag, it may have been that the

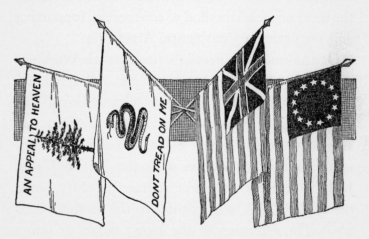

The Pine Tree and Rattlesnake Flags Were Popular Before the Outbreak of the Revolution and Continued in Use with Variations Through a Great Part of the Conflict. The Grand Union Flag Came into Being at the Beginning of 1776 but Was Soon Discarded. Then Came The Stars and Stripes.

stripes on his own escutcheon suggested them to the mind of Washington."

However this may be, the American Commander did not wait for Congress to act on the Grand Union Flag, and it was soon in common though not general use. In fact, there is no mention in the journals of Congress that the design was ever discussed by them in session. The entire flag subject was evidently not one of such importance in the minds of Congress as it was in Washington's.

In the spring of 1776, we find other banners still in use—whether due to the slow transmission of orders or to unpopularity of the Cambridge Flag, we do not know. Colonel Moultrie, in June, was still flying his blue flag with the silver crescent, and with the word "Liberty" blazoned on it, at Fort Sullivan, when he drove the British fleet out of the Charleston harbor. In February, Colonel Gadsden, a member of the Marine Committee in Philadelphia, the committee records state, "prefented to Congrefs an elegant ftandard fuch as is to be ufed by the Commander in Chief of the American navy; being a yellow flag with a rattle-fnake in the middle in the attitude of going to ftrike, and thefe words underneath, 'Don't tread on me.' Congrefs ordered that the faid ftandard be carefully preferved and fufpended in the Congrefs room." But if this design was actually used by the navy, Congress does not so state.

The origin of the rattlesnake as a symbol in early flags can only be conjectured. In *Bradford's Pennsylvania Journal* of December 27, 1775, a writer whose name is not known, and in some quarters was supposed to have been Franklin himself, discussed the possible reasons for its use.

. . . The rattlefnake is found in no other quarter of the globe than America, and may have therefore been chofen on that account. She never begins an attack, nor, when once engaged ever furrenders. She is therefore an emblem of magnanimity and true courage. . . . She never wounds until fhe has generoufly given notice even to her enemy, and cautioned him againft the danger of treading on her. Am I wrong, firs, in thinking this a ftrong picture of the temper and conduct of America?

At an earlier date, Doctor Franklin had published a cartoon representing the colonies as a serpent cut in thirteen segments, with the inscription, "Join or die."

When Washington left New York and hurried
to Philadelphia in response to the request of Congress, the flag problem was still on his mind.
The Grand Union Flag was not working out satis-
factorily. Evidently the thoughts of the colonies
were concentrating too strongly on separation
from England to permit the retention of the king's
colors. Ship captains, in particular, disliked them.

Regimental flags were also an urgent need.
Hardly had he reached Philadelphia, when he sent
a message to General Putnam, on this subject,
which is recorded in the American archives as
follows:

> After orders, May 31, 1776
> General Wafhington has written to General
> Putnam defiring him in the moft prefling terms to
> give pofitive orders to all the colonels to have
> colors immediately completed for their refpective
> regiments.

Colonel Ritzema, addressing the members of the
New York Provincial Congress the same date,
states that Washington's instructions were that
the banners be "of fuch a color and with fuch
devices as fhall be deemed proper by the [provin-
cial] Congrefs."

As we have seen, the commander in chief's first days in the Quaker City were taken up with the vital questions of organization to back up his defense against General Howe. Men were needed; supplies were needed. The tardiness of Congress must be overcome. We can imagine the strong mind and voice of Washington whipping the delegates to a sharp realization of the peril they would all be in if the delays continued.

During these busy days, the stalwart figure of the American leader was a familiar sight on Chestnut Street and High Street. With the sessions of Congress so crowded with supremely urgent matters, he sought opportunity to discuss other subjects dear to his heart with individual delegates outside. He knew all of these gentlemen—and their special capabilities. Robert Morris, the patriot financier, who later saved the American cause with his own private fortune, was chairman of the Secret Committee on military supplies. This committee met in the evenings and Washington was in frequent touch with it during his two weeks' stay in Philadelphia. Morris, owning many ships, was also an authority on marine affairs which the flag problem deeply concerned.

8

George Ross, a native of New Castle, Delaware, and now a delegate from Lancaster, Pennsylvania, was a lawyer of distinction, and had been thrown much in Washington's society during the first Continental Congress the preceding year.

To these two men, the commander in chief is believed to have confided his anxiety about a fitting national emblem to be used by the army and navy—and enlisted their aid. There is no record of their discussions or how they came to a decision on the general idea of the flag—but having reached it, the trio one day walked to the little shop of Betsy Ross the upholsterer, probably from the home of Robert Morris or perhaps from that of John Hancock at Fourth and Arch Streets, only a square away. They were in quest of assistance they knew without doubt she could render. George Ross had told his associates that if there was one woman in the city qualified more than another to help them in this emergency, it was his capable niece.

X

The Stars and Stripes

IT is a morning in early June. The linden trees spreading their branches over the Arch Street sidewalks are bright with fresh green foliage. The windows and doors of the tiny two-story shops are open to admit the spring air and sunshine. May had been cold and wet, and the sun's warm rays are doubly welcome.

Betsy Ross, having put away her breakfast things in her basement kitchen, is making ready for a busy day in the shop. There is much to be done. The usual interviews with callers; discussions of materials; the deft cutting and fitting and stitching all day long to please her patrons and keep a roof over her head.

Three gentlemen are observed standing at the door. Dropping her work, she steps forward to admit them. To her surprise, she sees Colonel George Ross, and beside him, too astounding for belief, she recognizes the tall, unmistakable figure of one who is talked about from end to end of the land—the leader of the Continental Army, General Washington! What has happened? she wonders. Robert Morris, too, whom she had so often seen driving through the streets—and marveled at his riches—now standing there with the other two—why on earth is he paying her a visit?

Bewildered indeed is this young widow as she hears the brief words of introduction and explanation from Colonel Ross—then, with rapidly beating heart, leads the way back through the crowded shop to her living room.

Like so many dwellings of the time, the ground floor of her home had but two rooms. At the front was the shop or office. At the rear, with painted walls and white sanded floor, and reached by a small connecting hallway, was the sitting room, which also did duty on formal occasions as dining room. Wall paper and carpets were then unknown except in the mansions of the wealthy. A winding stairway descended to the comfortable basement kitchen with its great brick fireplace, its wide hearth, and its brass and iron pots suspended from a stout swinging crane. Both the living room and the kitchen opened directly into a back yard which extended around to the side of the house.

Bewildered, She Hears the Words of Introduction by Colonel Ross

"Won't you be seated?" asked Mrs. Ross, her composure gradually returning—and placed a chair for General Washington.

It was not the first time, by any means, that she had seen the patriot commander, but probably the very first she had been in his presence. He stood six feet three inches tall, and there was something in the majesty and symmetry of his figure which made him look even taller. His head, with freshly powdered hair, seemed almost to touch the low ceiling. But cordiality shone from the depths of his blue eyes—as blue as her own—and his gracious voice and manner soon placed her completely at her ease.

The observing glances of her visitors took in the spotless and inviting appearance of Betsy Ross's modest home. It reflected her skill at her trade. At one end of the tiny room in which they sat, was a large fireplace and white mantelpiece framed in blue Dutch tile, with two tall brass candlesticks which showed plenty of evidence of vigorous polishing. A mahogany corner cupboard revealed shelves of glistening china, and at the side of the room was a small drop-leaf dining table which stood against the wall when not in use.

Through the open east windows, with their dainty hangings, the sun poured its golden rays, and the twitter of birds, busy at their own home-making, was heard in the little flower garden outside.

Nor did the neatly kept house alone attract the approving glances of the visitors. The charm of the one who made her abode here, as she sat facing them in her pretty cap and apron, her cheeks flushed, awaiting their pleasure, without doubt had its impression upon their masculine minds and added to the interest of their mission.

General Washington lost no time, however, in getting at the business of the moment. He drew from his pocket a sheet of paper showing a rough design of a flag with thirteen stripes and thirteen stars. Spreading it out on the table, he asked Mrs. Ross if she thought she could reproduce the same in bunting and secure an effective arrangement of the red, the white, and the blue. She inspected it for an instant and replied that she did not know but would gladly try.

Then noting that the stars in the design were six pointed, she quickly volunteered, "But I think the correct star should have five points." The General and his companions agreed with her, but said they felt that a six-pointed star could be more easily made, and that a large number of flags might soon be required. To this Mrs. Ross responded by deftly folding a scrap of paper in a certain manner—then with a single clip of her scissors she displayed to the astonished eyes of the committee a symmetrical five-pointed star.

This at once determined the point in her favor and other particulars were then discussed and agreed upon. The flag was to be made with red stripes at top and bottom, making seven red and six white stripes. The canton or union was to be a blue square, and in this blue field the thirteen white stars were to be arranged in the form of a circle.

How soon could she finish the flag? Betsy was asked as her visitors rose to go. "Very quickly," she replied. She would put aside other things and begin the task at once.

Thus was the matter decided. The interview was at an end. A brief and simple interview, but one with such portent that tens of thousands of citizens of a nation grown to be the mightiest in the world now come each year from near and far to see that little room.

Thanking Betsy profusely and bidding her do everything possible to hasten the work, the three statesmen took their departure.

With what tremors of suppressed excitement must she have watched them striding up the street! The great Washington had thus deigned to honor her humble abode—a fact which doubtless seemed vastly more important to her at the moment than the flag commission.

She had never before made a flag. But this did not disconcert her. It had been suggested that for her guidance in the peculiar stitch and hem, she call at the counting house of Mr. Morris on the water front and secure a sample of a ship's color. This she did, and as she related afterward, an old flag was drawn from a chest in the office and handed to her. She carefully examined its make-up—its extra rows of stitching at the seams, its heavy sailcloth binding at the side with strongly sewn eyelets for attachment to staff or peak. She was told to take it with her if she wished. On her way home, she stopped at a supply store for some bunting, and was soon hard at work on her task.

Far into the night she toiled in her candle-lighted living room—and again when morning dawned. Thus it was that by the following day her fast-flying fingers completed the first sample of Old Glory.

Straightway she notified Colonel Ross and Mr. Morris, who, in complimentary terms, expressed complete satisfaction with the flag. They praised her skill and her promptness; they told her they might require her assistance further— and doubtless, before they departed with the banner of red, white, and blue, she had to show them again the fascinating trick of making a five-pointed star with one snip of the scissors. They would soon let her know General Washington's opinion, they said.

XI

The Trial Period

ACCORDING to her statements in after years to her daughters, Colonel Ross returned a day or so later with the information that the design had been accepted. He also gave her a sum of money to defray expenses and directed her to make up a number of additional flags.

What became of that first design of the Stars and Stripes made in the shop of Betsy Ross?

The answer to this question has never been revealed. It will doubtless remain a mystery.

General Washington a few days later had to cut short his Philadelphia visit and hasten back to the army. The British were closing in on New York by land and sea. Any hour the attack would come.

Whether he had no time to bring the new flag design before Congress or whether he thought it best to wait until it had a tryout of popularity with his officers before formal adoption, we do not know. The latter is believed likely, though

Washington's diary and the records of Congress are as silent on this subject as they were on the Grand Union Flag which was designed at Cambridge and later discarded.

At all events, Betsy Ross continued the making of flags, and while the Stars and Stripes was not officially declared the national emblem by Congress until a year later, June 14, 1777, there is strong evidence that the new banner was in use in the meantime. In the Revolutionary archives of Pennsylvania, in the minutes of the State Navy Board, we read the following brief but significant paragraph with reference to her handiwork:

> State Navy Board, May 29th, 1777. Prefent, William Bradford, Jofeph Marfh, Jofeph Blewer, Paul Cox. An order on William Webb to Elizabeth Rofs, for fourteen pounds, twelve fhillings, two pence for making fhips' colours for William Richards' ftore.
>
> 14, 12, 2

Just when these particular colors were made and delivered is not stated, but from the deliberateness with which such committees usually acted, it was probably some weeks prior to the date of this order for payment.

Present   State Navy Board May 29th 1777
William Bradford C. M.   Joseph Marsh
Joseph Blewer   Paul Cox

An Order on William Webb to pay William and James Stuart, Seventeen Pounds ten Shillings for the freight of Seventy Perches of Stone from Schuylkill to the Piers for the Use of the Chevaux de Frize   at 5/ ℀ Perch . . . . . . £17. 10. c

An Order on William Webb to Pay Capt. Thomas Moore, Thirty Seven Pounds ten Shillings for Bounty Money ℀ Order from Commodore Hazelwood £37. 10.

An Order to Jacob Grantham to deliver Captain Stoddard of the Experiment Galley One Hundred and Fifty Weight of Junk

An Order on William Webb to Elizabeth Ross for fourteen Pounds Twelve Shillings and two Pence for Making Ships Colours &c Put into William Richards Store . . . . . — £14. 12. 2

PHOTOGRAPHIC REPRODUCTION OF ORIGINAL MINUTES OF THE PENNSYL-
VANIA STATE NAVY BOARD OF MAY 29, 1777, INCLUDING ORDER FOR
PAYMENT TO BETSY ROSS. THE PENNSYLVANIA ARCHIVES, REFERRING
TO THIS, STATE, "THE FIRST COLORS MADE FOR THE FLEET THAT WE
HAVE ANY RECORD OF WERE MADE BY ELIZABETH ROSS OF PHILADELPHIA."

According to a story in circulation in later years, the first Star-Spangled Banner made by Mrs. Ross was hoisted to the mast of a ship lying at Race Street wharf as an experiment. The above record gives some credence to this report and indicates in any event that one of the earliest demands for her services was for flags for the navy or merchant marine.

The *Pennsylvania Packet* of July 8, 1777, in describing a celebration held on the first anniversary of the Declaration of Independence, four days previously, says:

> About noon, all the armed fhips and galleys on the river were drawn up before the city, dressed in the gayeft manner, with the colours of the United States and ftreamers difplayed.

Who can doubt that the colors for which Betsy Ross was paid five weeks before played their part in that gala affair?

That the flags purchased from her for the supply store of William Richards were national and not state colors is regarded as highly probable, because Pennsylvania had no state flag until twenty-two years later—and no flag at all as a colony.

From whom came the first suggestion of the Stars and Stripes which prompted the design supplied to Betsy Ross? This question also will probably never be answered definitely. It may have been Washington's own idea to replace the Union Jack with the thirteen stars embodied in early Rhode Island banners.

For the first mention of a star in connection with a flag in the colonies, we have to go back to 1774, when a bit of verse was published in a little paper called the *Massachusetts Spy*.

> A ray of bright glory
>   Now gleams from afar;
> The American enfign
>   Now fparkles a ftar.

Captain John Manley, a Massachusetts shipowner, was inspired by this poem immediately afterward to design a flag with thirteen white stars on a blue union, with a blue anchor and the word "Hope" on a blue field. From this banner, those of a similar design which were carried by Rhode Island regiments at the start of the war were patterned.

It is declared by some authorities that Colonel Ross was really responsible for the combination of the Stars and Stripes. He was a noted lawyer, a great student, and was deeply interested in heraldry. Washington's coach had emblazoned on it his coat of arms, involving a white shield with three red stars at the top and two red stripes below, and for a crest an eagle rising out of a ducal coronet. These arms, it has been said, gave Colonel Ross his inspiration, and the suggestion of combining the stars and stripes in the new flag was concurred in by Robert Morris and received Washington's approval. It has also been contended that Francis Hopkinson, chairman of the Navy Board, who was likewise greatly interested in heraldry, was the first to suggest the new design.

General Washington did not set foot in Philadelphia again for more than a year. During that period the final decision on the flag remained in abeyance. In all important campaign matters, he sought the advice of his officers. Frequently in deciding some knotty problem or planning a battle, he would have every general present write his opinion on a slip of paper and hand it in. He would then render his decision. It would not be strange, therefore, if with the experiences of the

Grand Union and other flags in his mind, he should have believed actual usage to be a necessary test of the new design for the national emblem.

Congress at that time was but little more than an interstate council of safety. It proceeded mainly by way of advice and looked to the States rather than itself as the ultimate sources of authority. Throughout the war it was guided largely by Washington's judgment. He had put through the Grand Union Flag without its approval and probably did the same with the Stars and Stripes.

In after life, Betsy Ross fixed the date of her interview with the Flag Committee as "shortly before the Declaration of Independence." She could not remember the exact day and had made no note of it—but of one thing she was certain, the memorable signing of the Declaration came soon afterward. Her recollection is borne out by the dates of Washington's visit to Philadelphia in the spring of 1776, the only period he was in the city of Penn from the time he was made commander in chief until August, 1777, when the British were advancing to capture it.

XII

Old Glory's Baptism

AT the southwest corner of Seventh and High Streets, during the Revolution, stood a three-story brick house in which there lived a newly married couple named Graaf. They had a lodger, a tall, slender young man, thirty-three years old, with a determined chin, prominent cheek bones, freckles, and red hair. His name was Thomas Jefferson. He was a delegate to the Continental Congress from Virginia. As he himself afterward related, he rented the second floor of the house, "on the outſkirts of the town," ready furnished, upon his arrival in Philadelphia.

Let us now go back to the vivid events of 1776. During the warm June days after General Washington had hurried away to the army at New York, Jefferson sat much in his parlor and wrote and rewrote. He was crowding into one short document the ideas and aspirations which impelled the thirteen colonies to make a complete and final exit from the British Empire.

9

In the State House on Chestnut Street, his perspiring colleagues were discussing behind closed doors what John Adams pronounced, "the greatest question ever debated in America, and as great as ever was or will be debated among men."

Early in June, Richard Henry Lee, of Virginia, had introduced a resolution that "thefe United Colonies are and of right ought to be, free and independent States." On the first of July, Jeffer-

IN THE STATE HOUSE (INDEPENDENCE HALL) THE PERSPIRING DELEGATES WERE DISCUSSING "THE GREATEST QUESTION EVER DEBATED IN AMERICA"

son offered to Congress his Declaration of Independence. It had taken him eighteen days to finish it. Appointed to the Declaration Committee, as they told him, "because of his peculiar felicity of expression," he realized that it was the most important task of his life. Frequently, as he went along, he submitted his work to his fellow committeemen—Adams, Franklin, Roger Sherman, and Robert R. Livingston. The draft in Jefferson's handwriting as presented to Congress, which is still in existence, shows minor alterations in the penmanship of Franklin and Adams.

For three days Congress was torn by caustic debate over Jefferson's document, while the city waited in suspense. Everyone knew that something tremendous was happening, though few knew exactly its status. The proceedings were supposed to be secret, but there were many leaks and many wild rumors. Groups of the curious hung about the State House to catch glimpses of the bewigged and powdered delegates passing in and out. Thirst or fatigue often overcame the statesmen during those torrid days, and when that occurred they were seen hurrying across Chestnut Street in twos and threes to the hospitable State House

Inn, a solitary building in the middle of the block, shaded by spreading walnut trees. There, over the polished tables, they continued their argument in violent undertone or soothed their throats for coming oratorical efforts. And in the stables of John Nicholson, at the Indian Queen over in High Street, post horses were kept saddled in readiness to speed the final verdict to the waiting colonies.

How thrilling all this must have been to a young woman living in Arch Street, whose patriotic brain eagerly followed each move made in the gigantic game going on between America and England, and who had so recently figured in the designing of a proposed emblem for the struggling colonies! In common with her friends, Betsy Ross often went out of her way on her market rounds those extraordinary days to walk up Chestnut Street past the State House, drawn by the fascination surrounding the great men gathered there. The fact that she knew so many of them by sight from the time when they had first assembled in her father's beloved Carpenters' Hall, stimulated her interest in the part each was playing.

John Adams, the impetuous and portly New Englander, who had criticized most Jefferson's

work in the writing, became its champion on the
State House floor.   Jefferson, marvelously gifted
with his pen, had no speech-making powers.   He
sat silent and writhed while certain of the delegates
attacked his phraseology, and trusted to the elo-
quence of Adams to win them over.   And win them
it did, save for a few minor changes in the Declaration, which left it in no way weakened.

When, on the afternoon of July fourth, the Liberty Bell and the chimes of Christ Church broke
into a loud and joyful chorus, nobody was long
in the dark as to what had happened.   People
swarmed excitedly toward Chestnut Street.   Expresses raced from the city to General Washington
and the colonial capitals.   The Tories, locking
themselves in their homes and countinghouses to
escape the taunts of exulting patriots, in many
cases had to dodge stronger expressions which
came their way in the form of bricks sent crashing
through their windows.

While the Declaration was adopted July fourth,
there was no official celebration that day.   The
big time was reserved for the following Monday,
July eighth.   By that morning, the document had
been neatly set in type around at the printshop of

Dunlap and Claypoole in High Street, and it was then formally proclaimed to the people.

From a platform erected in the State House yard, now Independence Square, the stentorian tones of Sheriff John Nixon carried the words almost to the far corners of the square. There were no electric amplifiers for public speakers in those days, but from all accounts, none was needed on that occasion. Nixon's lung power, which prompted his selection for the part, was entirely adequate.

The ringing of the Liberty Bell and the church bells for an hour beforehand called the people together, and should anyone today be in doubt as to whether Philadelphians attached importance to that event, let him read the following from the diary of one Christopher Marshall of the Committee of Safety:

July 8. At eleven, went and met committee of Inspection at Philosophical Hall; went from there in a body to the Lodge; joined the Committee of Safety. Went in a body to the State House Yard, where in the presence of a great concourse of people, the Declaration of Independence was read by John Nixon. The company declared their approbation by three repeated huzzas. The King's Arms were taken down in the court room and State House at the fame time.

I went and dined at Paul Fook's. Then he and the French Engineer went with me on the Commons, where the fame was proclaimed to each of the five battalions. There were bonfires, ringing bells and other demonftrations of joy upon the unanimity and agreement of the Declaration.

And so, the new nation was given a send-off which no one soon forgot. Through the veins of Betsy Ross, as she listened to the speeches and joined in the celebration that day and evening, there must have surged emotions a-plenty, particularly as she recalled the little drama of the flag enacted at her home a short month before. And in the days which followed, as she continued to fashion bunting in increasing quantities into red, white, and blue banners, she heard with interest all the more intense each scrap of news which trickled in from Washington's little army, face to face with the well-trained troops of Lord Howe.

The news was anything but encouraging for months to come. The Declaration, which was expected to hearten the Continental soldiers, seemed to be the signal for a series of disasters.

Defeated in a desperately fought battle on Long Island, Washington abandoned New York to the combined British and Hessian forces. His fall campaign to dislodge them was a failure, and with the first snows of December, all Philadelphia was frightened to hear that he was retreating southward across New Jersey with the enemy in full pursuit. The British intentions were obvious. They were determined to capture the "ragamuffin army of Mr. Washington," as they termed his three thousand underfed, underpaid troops, then descend on Philadelphia, and end the war.

Prayers of thanksgiving arose in the Quaker City when it was learned that Washington had succeeded in placing the Delaware between himself and his pursuers at the village of Trenton— and then the day after Christmas came word which set the whole town wild with rejoicing. Washington had recrossed the river in a storm of sleet during the night, had fallen upon the Hessians under Colonel Rall, who was merrymaking in Trenton, and had captured over a thousand men, practically the entire force. As if this were not enough glad news, they learned the following week that Washington had boldly marched against a division of Lord Cornwallis himself, at Princeton, and after a bloody conflict had actually driven the British from the field.

Glorious tidings indeed! But tidings that were tempered with sadness, for the bells of Christ Church which had tolled in solemn requiem for so many Philadelphians in the past year now rang during the burial of General Hugh Mercer, who was slain while leading a charge against Cornwallis. To Betsy Ross there seemed to be a never-ending march of funerals along Arch Street—a ceaseless beat of muffled drums past her windows.

But Trenton and Princeton! They thrilled her. Ranked among the decisive battles of history, these victories were the first real revelations of Washington's military genius since his early experiences in the Indian wars. Distrusted by many of his followers, despised by the British, he had astounded both by his New Jersey maneuvers and now became the idol of the patriot army.

"All our hopes were blasted by that unhappy affair at Trenton," exclaimed Lord George Germain, the king's Secretary of State for the Colonies, in a speech to his anxious colleagues in the House of Commons two years later.

Curiously enough, Trenton and Princeton, which had so much to do with the final triumph of the American arms, have brought down to us interesting light on an important question—as to when the Betsy Ross design of Stars and Stripes first saw actual combat—a subject about which there has been a century-old controversy.

At these two engagements there was a young captain of infantry—Charles Willson Peale. He was also an artist of distinction. Through a great part of the war, he painted while he fought—long hours in camp being devoted to brush and palette. Two noted portraits by Peale of Washington on the battle field of Princeton bear directly on the flag question.

The first of these he began at the request of Congress the same year as the Princeton victory —while the army was encamped at Valley Forge— and finished it a year later. It depicts the patriot commander at the close of the battle, with captured enemy flags grouped at his feet and a flag with a circlet of thirteen stars in a blue field waving overhead. The starry banner is at the extreme edge of the painting—and the stripes, if stripes were intended, are thus cut off from view.

As though to atone for this slight to the stripes, Peale, in 1783, gave them special prominence in his second full-length portrait, "Washington at the Battle of Princeton." Nassau Hall, of the College of New Jersey, is shown in the background with the conflict swirling about it. General Mercer is stretched dying on the ground, and over Washington's head a color bearer holds a huge flag with thirteen stripes and a glimpse of a blue field in which stars faintly but unmistakably glimmer.

The first of these Peale portraits now hangs in the Senate gallery at Washington and the second is the prized possession of Princeton University.

Another soldier artist, equally noted, was inspired by Trenton and Princeton to give us similar records on canvas. John Trumbull, son of the Revolutionary governor of Connecticut, was Washington's aide-de-camp at the start of the war, fought valiantly at Crown Point and Ticonderoga, and remained in active service until February, 1777. Soon after the war ended, there came from his brush three pictures now world-famous: "The Battle of Trenton," showing Washington on horseback, looking compassionately down at the dying Hessian, Colonel Rall; a standing full-length portrait of the American leader, entitled "General Washington at the Battle of Trenton," and "The Death of General Mercer at the Battle of Princeton." The last named depicts the fallen Philadelphian about to be bayoneted by a British grenadier, with Washington a short distance away at the head of his troops, over whom floats the flag of thirteen stripes and thirteen stars. In all three of these Trumbull paintings this flag is a conspicuous feature.

Peale and Trumbull, renowned artists of the Revolution, were both known for their fidelity to historical details. It was the latter's custom in all his war paintings to complete first the composition and details, leaving out the heads, which he filled in from life as opportunity offered. He went to great lengths to secure sittings from the generals involved. In his *Reminiscences*, the artist states that he painted the portraits of General Washington into his canvases at sittings in New York. One of these occasions was probably March 2, 1790, for under that date, the following appears in Washington's diary:

Sat for Mr. Trumbull to paint my likeneſs into his Hiſtorical Scenes.

The accuracy of the paintings is thus largely confirmed.   Had the flags depicted by Trumbull been wrong, the quick eye of Washington would doubtless have detected the error.   It is regarded as extremely probable, moreover, that the artist and his former commander, who knew each other intimately, discussed such features at the sittings with a view to having them correct in all particulars.

Another equally famous picture by Trumbull, "The Battle of Bunker's Hill," fought in June, 1775, shows the New England Pine Tree flag used by the Continental troops at that engagement—significant in its proof of the artist's scrupulous attention to flag accuracy.   It was Trumbull's unusual regard for authenticity as well as his skill which called forth Washington's praise for his paintings on more than one occasion.

That Charles Willson Peale's first portrait of "Washington at Princeton," was proof positive that the emblem shown on the canvas waved over the victorious Americans that January day in New Jersey, was believed by the artist's son, Titian R. Peale.   In a letter written on this subject some time after the Revolution, he said, "The flag represented is a blue field with white stars arranged in a circle. I don't know that I ever heard my father speak of that flag, but the trophies at Washington's feet I know he painted from the flags then captured and which were left with him for that purpose. He was always very particular in matters of historical record in his pictures." The letter adds that he is sure that the flag represented was not a regimental flag, but "one to mark the new republic."

From correspondence later between Washington and the Board of War, we are led to believe that the Stars and Stripes was not then—or even after its adoption by Congress—distributed to the various regiments as their standard emblem. Neither, however, was any other banner supplied by Congress. Apparently the new flag was designated chiefly as a marine banner, though the official seal of the War Board used in the Revolution clearly shows its recognition also as an army symbol, with the stars, however, in rectangular form instead of a circle. The paintings of Trumbull and Peale, which may be classed as contemporary records, indicate that, in both forms, it saw service soon after the act of separation from

England; that Washington brought the new emblem to the attention of his leaders, and employed it at Trenton and Princeton—and this six months before its formal approval by Congress! A circumstance which checks with the statement of Betsy Ross that the flag was actually born in the year 1776.

With the Declaration of Independence, the Union Jack or King's Colors, had quickly vanished from the American banner—almost as quickly as the King's Arms were torn down and burned at the State House and other public buildings through the colonies. The Stars and Stripes was designed as the successor of the Grand Union Flag— and Trumbull and Peale, soldiers of the Revolution, have handed down records which give a strong impression that it had its baptism in battle at those crucial engagements in New Jersey.

OFFICIAL SEAL OF BOARD OF WAR, DE-SIGNED IN 1778, AND IN CONTINUOUS USE, FEATURING STARS AND STRIPES.

XIII

Congress Approves

A S the spring came on, British thoughts again centered on Philadelphia. Angered by Washington's winter exploits, General Howe laid new plans to seize the rebel capital and end the business once and for all. Besides, he had heard much of the gay life among the rich Tories in the city on the Delaware, and a glimpse of it strongly appealed to Sir William as a pleasant wind-up of his American experiences.

Congress was very much alive to his intentions and redoubled its efforts toward a larger and better equipped fighting force. Recruiting was speeded up by the Committee of Safety through the city and in the rural districts. Betsy Ross, busy at her flag-making, saw increasing numbers of her acquaintances devoting themselves to their country's service on land and sea.

There were two of these—John Claypoole and Joe Ashburn—in whom she had more than a passing interest, dating from their school days, and who, as events proved, were to resume very active interest in her. In fact, it was about this time that rumors which caused almost as much talk as the war, in her neighborhood, began to be circulated in which her name was associated with the popular sea captain's. Between voyages in his trading vessel, he had taken up the broken threads of his friendship with the young and attractive widow, calling very often at her Arch Street shop, and not always, it was suspected, to purchase colors for his ship.

Both Ashburn and Claypoole, it will be recalled, were among those Betsy Griscom had favored most in the old peace-time days when they had organized sailing or fishing parties on the Delaware or all-day picnics into the country. Both were keen rivals for her hand up to the time John Ross had walked off with her affections.

From his boyhood Joe Ashburn had virtually lived on and in the water. His companions used to marvel at his skill with an oar or the tiller of his catboat, and at the easy grace with which he swam to the New Jersey side of the broad river and back. As he grew older, he made several voyages before the mast, and when he was twenty-one his aunt,

10

Mrs. Ashburn, placed him in command of the *Swallow*, a brig in which she was a principal owner, engaged in the West Indian trade.

Of late, Ashburn and Claypoole had seen but little of each other or of Betsy, for while the former was sailing the seas in the merchant marine, Claypoole was marching and drilling with the Pennsylvania militia. Occasionally Betsy had had glimpses of John when visiting his sisters, but he was apparently too full of the business of war to give either her or them more than a passing thought.

Fate had decreed, however, that the old intimacy of these two young men was to be renewed in a manner none of them expected. Far across the seas, they were to come together under extraordinary circumstances—with Betsy Ross, friend of their youth, destined to be the third figure in a strange triangle of tragedy and romance growing out of the war.

The voyages of Ashburn and his fellow skippers were becoming more and more important to the struggling nation—and also, for the same reason, more hazardous. Supplies of all kinds were desperately needed, and each shipload, particularly of munitions, that came in, was worth its weight in gold. Of this the enemy was fully aware, and British frigates and privateers made it their special business to lie in wait for the American merchantmen along the coast. Their threats soon led all trading vessels to carry guns to protect themselves, and many an earnest chase by his majesty's ships was spoiled by the rapidly improving marksmanship of the rebel sailors.

The glamour of the sea held sway over feminine hearts then as always. Captain Ashburn, young, broad-shouldered, strong-willed, was an impetuous

They Were Married June 15, at Wicaco, in Old Swedes' Church

wooer. He is described in the old shipping files of Pennsylvania as "five feet eight inches tall, of a fair complexion," and, in that eventful year 1777, twenty-six years of age, one year Betsy's senior. And when it finally became known that he had won her consent to be his wife, there were few who criticized or made comment other than to give them every good wish.

Those were days of brief widowhoods, as the marriage records show. Not far from the home of Mrs. Ross, a few years later, lived another daughter of the Quakers, Dolly Payne Todd, who had moved there from Virginia. It was less than a year after the death of her husband, John Todd, a young Philadelphia lawyer, that she wedded James Madison, at that time a delegate to Congress from Virginia, and thus became the Dolly Madison of White House fame.

Betsy Ross and Joseph Ashburn, on June 15, went down to "Wicaco," as the Indians had called the wooded district south of the city, and there were married by the Rev. Andrew Goeranson, rector of Gloria Dei (Old Swedes') Church. Many of their friends attended the ceremony in this quaint house of worship—the oldest church

Knight Gilbert and Mary Grames May the 8

James Ward and Eleanor Loveley May the 8

John Burk and Eleanor Cherry May the 8

John Weaver and Jean Davis May the 28

Richard Page and Mary Winters May the 8

Benjamin Rue and Mary Paybon May
        the 29 by Licence

Firanius Jones and Mary Brooks May
        the 30 —

James McDole and Eleanor Hughes
        June the 6 —

Edward Rowan & Elizabeth Cox
        June the 8 by Licence

Martin Murphey and Hannah Smith
        June the 8 —

Henry Abbot & Elizabeth Marshall June
        the 9 —

John Hitton and Elizabeth Page June the 9

Edward Flinn & Sarah Johnson June the 11

William Dudley & Mary Bryant June the
        11 by Licence —

James Gold & Elizabeth Clemons June the 13

Joseph Ashburn and Elizabeth Ross
        June the 15 by Licence —

William Clark and Prischila Peercer June
        the 16 —

PAGE 61, BOOK OF MARRIAGE RECORDS, OLD SWEDES' CHURCH, 1777,
RECORDING MARRIAGE OF JOSEPH ASHBURN AND ELIZABETH ROSS, BY
LICENSE. IN SOME CASES WEDDINGS WERE BY PUBLISHED BANS AND
IN OTHERS BY LICENSE

in Philadelphia—overlooking the Delaware, and the young couple then took up their abode in the bride's Arch Street home.

That she should continue the duties of her little shop it was decided as a matter of course. Important as was her husband's vocation on the sea, which threatened to take him away from her for weeks at a time, her own was just as important or more so. They were entirely agreed on that point.

By a singular coincidence, their wedding took place on the very next day after Congress passed a resolution, in which, had she known of it, she would have been greatly interested. The resolution officially approved as the national banner the Stars and Stripes which she had helped to fashion a whole year before.

In the handwriting of Charles Thomson, Secretary, under date of June 14, 1777, the journals of Congress contain this brief paragraph tucked away amid many others:

> *Reſolved—That the Flag of the united ſtates ~~conſiſt of~~ be ~~diſtinguiſhed by~~ 13 ſtripes alternate red and white, that the Union be 13 ſtars white in a blue field repreſenting a new conſtellation.*

What brought the resolution about at this particular time is not known. There is no record of debates or any preliminary discussion by Congress on the subject. It was a time, however, of rushed preparations to meet the enemy's attack. Lord Howe, it was expected, would come by water. Washington was planning to thwart him if possible, and Congress was giving every coöperation in its power.

There were many measures passed June 14, according to the crowded pages of the journal, and the flag adoption was sandwiched in between resolutions pertaining to the fleet, all in the Thomson handwriting. One resolution gave the Marine Committee power to take such action "refpecting the continental fhips of war in the river Delaware as they think proper in cafe the enemy fucceed in their attempts on faid river." Two which followed suspended Captain John Roach from command of the ship of war *Ranger*, because of reports that he was "a perfon of doubtful character," and appointed Captain John Paul Jones to succeed him.

Other paragraphs immediately below these likewise related to fleet activity. They indicate that

Resolved That the marine committee be impowered to
give such directions respecting the continental
ships of war in the river Delaware as they
think proper in case the enemy succeed in
their attempts on the said River.

Resolved That the Flag of the united states consist
of 13 stripes alternate red and white, that the
Union be 13 stars white in a blue field representing a new constellation.

The Council of the state of Massachusetts bay
having represented by letter to the president
of Congress that capt John Roach sometime
since appointed to command the continental
ship of war the Ranger is a person of doubtful character and ought not to be intrusted
with such a command. therefore

Resolved That captain Roach be suspended
until the navy board for the eastern depart-
ment shall have inquired fully into his character & report thereon to the marine committee.

Resolved That capt John Paul Jones be appointed
to command the said ship Ranger.

Resolved That William Whipple esq. member
of Congress and of the marine committee
John Langdon esq. continental agent and
the said capt John Paul Jones be authorised

THE RECORD WHICH FIXES FLAG DAY. A PAGE FROM THE ORIGINAL
ROUGH JOURNAL OF CONGRESS, JUNE 14, 1777, SHOWING RESOLUTION
AUTHORIZING STARS AND STRIPES. SEVERAL WORDS CROSSED OUT IN
MAKING THE ENTRY INDICATE EITHER UNCERTAIN RECOLLECTION OF A
MEASURE PREVIOUSLY ADOPTED OR A VOTE SO HASTY THAT TIME WAS
NOT TAKEN TO WRITE OUT AND AGREE ON THE WORDING BEFOREHAND

General Howe's designs on the city were very much on the minds of Congress that day, and suggest that the flag vote was the hasty passage of a long delayed measure in order to give an official sanction to colors for the ships. Either this, or the paragraph was the hasty recording of a resolution passed some time previously. By some this is believed to have been the case, since the words crossed out give the impression that the correct phraseology was somewhat hazy in the mind of Charles Thomson as he entered it.

The State House had been apathetic toward many matters which Washington regarded as important, including the national emblem, and, in any event, it is highly probable that the flag resolution was held up far longer than he wished. Rear Admiral Preble, in his comprehensive book published in 1872 on the flag and its history, remarks:

This dilatory resolve of Congress, it will be observed, was not passed until eighteen months after the union flag-raising at Cambridge, and the sailing of the first American fleet from Philadelphia under Continental colors. Nearly a year after the declaration of the entire separation of the colonies from Great Britain, and another two and a half months elapsed before it was promulgated officially. There was red tape in those early days as well as now. No record of the discussions which undoubtedly preceded the adoption of the stars and stripes has been preserved.

By "another two and a half months," Preble refers to the fact that the flag resolution was not officially published in the newspapers until September 3, when merely the paragraph itself, unaccompanied by comment, appeared in the *Pennsylvania Gazette*, and in other places later. Apparently, the papers chose to make but a perfunctory reference to a flag design already familiar to them.

Following the act of June 14, however, and the newspaper notices, the use of the Stars and Stripes increased, particularly in the navy, and the little shop of Elizabeth Ross Ashburn became busier than ever. The popularity of the new design having been proved by actual use, Congressional indorsement caused its gradual adoption through the colonies, even though Congress itself, negligent in so many things, apparently took no steps to supply the colors in quantities. The ships and regiments were left to supply themselves as best they might with flags, often through their State governments. The distances were great and quick communication lacking; therefore it was some time before many were equipped.

But in the trying days soon to come—days when the hopes of Washington's followers fell to their lowest ebb—the Stars and Stripes served well in binding them closely together as brothers in the fight for freedom. In many a desperate struggle on the seas, nailed to the mastheads of schooners and brigs, it was to glorify the name of the young nation as a naval power. At Brandywine, Germantown, and Valley Forge, too, as many believe, this new emblem waved with other flags and cheered the patriot troops amid reverses.

"We take the stars from heaven," the American commander once said in expressing the sentiment conveyed by the new flag. "We take the red from our mother country, separating it by white stripes, thus showing that we have separated from her, and the white stripes shall go down to posterity representing Liberty."

What led to the decision to confine the Stars and Stripes primarily to marine use is today a mooted question. The wording of the act of

Congress approving the design and terming it the "flag of the United States" indicates an intention to make it the symbol of the entire country. That may have been Washington's idea at first. If so, the records indicate a change of thought, for as late as May, 1779, we find uncertainty on the subject, and the Board of War writing the commander asking his advices as to a "standard for the various regiments." This is the more puzzling in view of the War Board's official seal, then in use, which includes the Stars and Stripes as part of its design.

For many years England had used different flags for her naval and land forces. This may have influenced Washington to draw a distinction between his own. It is worthy of note that the Grand Union Flag which he had brought into being at Boston was patterned after the British marine flag of that day, and was used primarily in the navy.

June 14, the date on which the Continental Congress officially recognized the Betsy Ross design, is the one which America now celebrates as Flag Day, in the absence of definite knowledge as to the exact date of that other June day which saw the actual conception of the Star-Spangled Banner.

XIV

The Quaker Exiles

ONE afternoon in August, General Howe put
to sea, his transports packed with redcoats,
supposedly headed for Delaware Bay. A huge
fleet of 228 sail and 19,000 men! He left Sir
Henry Clinton in command of New York.

As far as the eye could see, the white sails
dotted the waters of the harbor as this stupendous
armada got under way—a startling spectacle for
Yankee scouts peering from the wooded heights
of the shore.

Washington hurried down from northern New
Jersey and pitched his camp at Germantown,
which was then a small village six miles from Philadelphia. There he awaited developments, rapidly
recruiting his army and planning with Congress
to give the visitors the warmest possible reception.

When word came that instead of entering the
Delaware, the British had sailed up the Chesa-
peake and were marching northward from the
head of the bay, he hastened to meet them. On

his way, however, he decided to parade his entire army through the capital and make as brave a display as possible to reassure its frightened citizens.

Reassurance was sadly needed. Business was at a standstill. Whigs were feverishly packing their belongings in readiness to flee, or were busy with spades in back yards burying silverware, jewels, and money. Congress itself made ready for a quick exit, so dubious was it of Washington's chances. But everybody, nevertheless, turned out as on a holiday to see Philadelphia's first parade of the Continental Army.

To Betsy Ross Ashburn, consumed by hopes for the patriot cause, that parade was a red-letter event never to be effaced from her memory—a sight that thrilled her whole being, while it saddened her in the vague dread of the coming conflict.

Eleven thousand men, stepping briskly to the strains of "Yankee Doodle," she saw marching from the dusty Germantown highroad into the city. Men whose bronzed cheeks told a story of life on farms, on fishing boats, and in lumber camps. Most of them in rough homespun—brown, blue, or buff, occasionally with red trimmings, according to the colors of their state militia;

some in white duck rifle shirts and leggings; all wearing a sprig of green in their cocked hats— pathetic touch to give them a more jaunty and uniform appearance.

To the piercing notes of the fife, many sang as they marched, down Front Street and into Chestnut, their chorus swelling to a mighty shout as they neared the State House where members of Congress and their families stood looking on. . . .

> "*Yankee Doodle went to town.*
> *He rode upon a pony.*
> *He stuck a feather in his cap,*
> *And called it macaroni.*
>
> "*Yankee Doodle, keep it up;*
> *Yankee Doodle dandy—*
> *Mind the music and the step,*
> *And with the girls be handy.*"

Washington was at their head. Beside him rode the youthful Lafayette, lately arrived from France. Close behind were others of whom Philadelphians had heard much, but few had seen; Knox and Greene and Sullivan; Lee and Alexander Hamilton; the fiery Anthony Wayne and the daredevil Colonel Moylan, each with Trenton and Princeton fresh in his mind and eager to repeat.

Quickly the long column disappeared toward the Schuylkill, crossing at Gray's Ferry—and while it was winding its way southward over the Baltimore Pike, the Delaware became the theater of battle preparations. That usually placid stream swirled with action. Howe's fleet would soon be coming up—of that everyone was certain.

Chevaux-de-frise, or spiked obstructions, were strung across the river. Brigs and schooners were arming and drilling their crews. Huge galleys, or "calevats," designed and built for just this emergency, were darting along the shore carrying supplies to Forts Mifflin and Mercer which guarded the channel below the city. Formidable fighting craft, too, were these galleys—fifty feet long and propelled by lusty oarsmen like the Roman ships of old. Swift, easily handled, they were armed with howitzers and bristled with pikes and muskets —and where there was not enough gunpowder to go around they were equipped with bows and arrows.

While Commodore Hazelwood was thus hurrying the Pennsylvania State Navy to a condition of preparedness, Doctor Benjamin Rush, America's eminent physician, appointed surgeon-general of the military hospitals, went flying about the streets in his phaëton, marshaling the city's medical men for the bloody battles that were coming.

Captain Joseph Ashburn, back from a trip to the Indies which followed his honeymoon, found plenty to do these tumultuous days. His knowledge of ships and shipping was put to good stead on the river. Betsy, too, was often down at the wharves, fascinated by the bustle and excitement. Many a brig and galley, freshly outfitted, flew at peak or stern a flag made at her busy shop.

Frequently her glance turned from the sweating, shouting sailormen to the Old Bank Meeting House as it stood frowning from the river bank upon these unholy steps toward conflict. She gazed reminiscently also, on meeting days, at the drab-garbed Friends passing in and out as of yore, closing their ears to the noise of the wharves.

Holding firmly to their peace ideas, they did their best to remain aloof from the war fever. But while Washington was marching to engage the enemy, a storm suddenly broke over their Society the like of which Quakerism had not experienced since its earliest days in Old England. So extraordinary was it indeed that it overshadowed for a period the British advance and made an impres-

11

sion on Elizabeth Ashburn which she never forgot.

One evening, she was brought to the door of her shop by a commotion in the street. She was astonished to see a richly dressed old gentleman in Quaker attire struggling in the hands of two Pennsylvania militiamen. His wide-brimmed beaver was reposing in the street, his ruffled shirt and wig were in disarray. On the sidewalk was a gathering throng of Friends of both sexes, angrily protesting.

As Betsy approached, she saw that the soldiers had hold of Israel Pemberton, a prominent member of the Meeting, and often called, because of his wealth and liberality, "The King of the Quakers."

"He has been arrested for refusing to take the oath of allegiance," someone told her.

As they vanished toward High Street and the City Hall, the whole neighborhood was thrown into excitement by the appearance of similar groups in various streets and alleys. Militiamen were entering the residences of leaders of the Meeting and placing them under arrest. Their families looked on in bewilderment. Frightened children ran through the streets spreading the news. To add to the alarm, rumors flew about that the accused Quakers were to be banished from the city.

A drastic move by the Pennsylvania legislature caused these arrests. With the approach of the British, the Tories had become so bold in their actions that a measure was passed requiring all inhabitants to take oath or affirmation of active allegiance to the United States and Pennsylvania, and renounce forever their connection with the king and government of Great Britain.

In the enforcement of this law, which so conflicted with the principles of their Society, prominent Quakers were inevitably drawn into the toils, with openly avowed Tories. While many of the younger members obeyed the decree, most of the leaders refused, and the more conspicuous of these were proceeded against as examples. Seeing an opportunity to vent their old grudge against the Quakers, the Episcopalians and Presbyterians, dominating the legislature, went after the very heads of the Bank Meeting and the Great Meeting at Second and High streets. Twenty of these, including Henry Drinker himself, of the Northern District, were locked up in the Lodge of the Free Masons, Filbert Street above Eighth.

Nothing in all the war's topsy-turvy events created more sensation than this, or was more astounding to the mind of Elizabeth Ashburn, who, despite her ostracism, and her belief that the Quakers were wrong in their war attitude, still looked upon the Friends' Meeting as the very center and bulwark of society. The revered Henry Drinker, Clerk of the Bank Meeting and member of the great importing house of James and Drinker, arrested like a common thief and about to be sent into exile! She could not believe it.

In the care of the Old Bank Meeting she had grown to womanhood. From the days when she was still a schoolgirl in short dresses, her hair in a long thick braid, she had looked up to Henry Drinker and his sweet-faced wife, the former Elizabeth Sandwith, as models of culture and virtue. To be sure, as head of the Meeting, he had been the leader in the disownment proceedings taken against her three years before, but there was no rancor in her heart over that inevitable sequel of her marriage—only sympathy now for the distraught Quaker families all about her. Something of the state of mind of these households may be gathered from a page in the journal of Elizabeth

Drinker herself, which she kept during the war and in which she describes her husband's plight:

Sept 2, 1777 (Third day)

H. D., *having been and continuing to be unwell, ſtayed from Meeting this morning. He went, toward noon, into yᵉ front parlor to copy the Monthly Meeting minutes—the book on yᵉ deſk, and yᵉ deſk unlocked, when William Bradford, one Blewer, and Ervin entered, offering a parole for him to ſign—which was refuſed. They then ſeized on yᵉ book and took ſeveral papers out of yᵉ deſk and carried them off, intimating their deſign of calling the next morning at 9 o'clock and deſiring H. D. to ſtay at home at that time, which as he was unwell, was unneceſſary. They accordingly called in yᵉ morning and took my Henry away to the Maſons' Lodge in an illegal, unprecedented manner, where are ſeveral other Friends with ſome of other perſuaſions made priſoners— Iſrael Pemberton, John Hunt, James Pemberton, John Pemberton, Thomas Wharton, Edward Pennington, Phineas Bond, Thomas Gilpin, Thomas Combe, Thomas Pike, Owen Jones, Jr., Thomas Affleck, Charles Jarvis, William Smith, [broker], William Druit Smith, Thomas Fiſher, Charles Eddy, Miers Fiſher and Samuel Pleaſants.*

I went this morning to ſee my H. D., where I met with yᵉ wives and children of our dear Friends, and with other viſitors, in great numbers.

Against Israel Pemberton and his two brothers, James and John, the legislature was especially severe. They stood in the van of those of their faith who had long battled against the proprietary governors of the province who were not so tender toward the Quaker interests as William Penn had been. Israel, who had served in the legislature, had been arrested once before for his violent criticisms of Governor George Thomas. James and John, like their brother, were wealthy merchants. They were among the founders of the Pennsylvania Hospital and were identified with many educational and philanthropic enterprises which had made the Quaker colony so influential in America.

This powerful group of Friends now employed every possible legal method to effect their release. Abel James, uncle of Elizabeth Ashburn—wealthy, influential, and the business partner of Henry Drinker—left no stone unturned to save him from the ignominy which threatened. Terming the action of the authorities "high-handed and unwarranted perfecution," they appealed to the members of Congress, who, however, declined to interfere. The Supreme Executive Council, representing the legislature, decreed that, without trial, they be exiled to a remote and unsettled section of Virginia because of "conduct inimical to the cause of America."

On the afternoon of September 11, the prisoners were told to bid farewell to their families—then placed in wagons and paraded through the streets on the start of their humiliating journey, while from the sidewalks the townsfolk stared at the extraordinary spectacle. Escorted southward by a guard of Light Horse, they were turned over to the governor of Virginia—to be confined for eight long months at the town of Winchester before appeals to General Washington finally set them free.

The Quakers and their condemnation of warfare as an immoral and uneconomic means of settling disputes brought about a unique situation in Pennsylvania. It was not that they were out of sympathy with the patriot party in endeavoring to right their country's wrongs, but they objected to war as the method. In reply to accusations against them, the Yearly Meeting declared that in refusing to join in warlike measures, they were simply obeying their consciences and the divine command, as they understood it, to live at peace with all men. Moreover, where God's command and human law seemed to be in opposition, they obeyed the higher law and willingly suffered the consequences whatever they might be.

In this firm stand, the Quakers had but little deterrent effect upon armed conflicts of their day, but apparently they were sowing the seeds of future harvest. Their peace testimony, so stead-fastly maintained for two centuries as part of their plan for a better social world, had its first great test in America in the French and Indian wars and its second in the Revolution. Mankind was not then ready for any such philosophy. History, however, will doubtless accord to the Friends a large measure of credit for thus helping to mold world consciousness. Just as they were pioneers for education and freedom of worship, those Quakers of olden times were also pioneers for principles which today, in the twentieth century, seem to point the way toward a new understanding among nations, and the uprooting of those ancient war traditions which George Fox and Penn opposed so vigorously.

XV

Cornwallis Enters

ON the very day that the procession of exiled Quakers and Tories filed slowly out of Philadelphia, the booming of guns to the southwest told everyone that the long dreaded hour had come. Washington and Howe were locked in battle.

The city trembled in uncertainty until late afternoon. Then expresses arrived with the terrifying intelligence that the British were completely victorious, and that the beautiful Brandywine Creek, twenty-five miles away, was running red with patriot blood. A panic followed. All night long, the wagons of fleeing Whigs, piled high with household goods, clattered over the cobblestone streets on their way to distant towns.

Congress also hurriedly departed. The dignified statesmen traveled as quickly as coaches and fast horses could carry them to Lancaster, seventy miles distant—and later to York, from which safe refuge they watched the mighty duel which went on between Lord Howe and the American commander. Sir William's forces outnumbered his opponent's almost two to one.

Washington's desperate appeal for troops brought the last reserves of militia of Pennsylvania and adjoining States on the run to join the main army. Officers were commissioned; new regiments were outfitted and rushed off to do their bit against the seasoned veterans of the king.

Among the minute men to receive a commission that memorable September was Private John Claypoole, with whom this narrative is largely concerned. For two years he had served in Philadelphia with but little activity except in the guarding of prisoners and stores and awaiting the chance to see real campaigning under General Washington. Brandywine brought him that opportunity. The war files record that September 13, 1777, "John Claypoole was commiſſioned a Second Lieutenant in Col. Jehu Eyre's regiment."

The Claypoole family from then on figured gallantly in the Revolution. With two of his cousins, Captain Abraham George Claypoole and Lieutenant David Chambers Claypoole, commissioned the same year, John served with distinction, adding to the luster of a name already prominent in the colony's history.

The great-grandfather of these three young men, James Claypoole, came to America in 1683 from the family home, Claypoole Manor, Norborough, England. His brother, John Claypoole, was the husband of Elizabeth Cromwell, daughter of Oliver Cromwell, Lord Protector of the Kingdom. James, a wealthy merchant, high in the councils of William Penn, received a grant of five thousand acres of land in the New World. Upon reaching Philadelphia, he built his home at what is now Second and Walnut streets on a lot covering one and one-quarter acres, with "greene lawns floping down to the pleafant Dock creek." This stream, long since blotted out by the city's growth, then had its source in a large pond near Fifth and High Streets and flowed in a southeasterly direction into the Delaware.

Prominent among the English Quakers, James at once became a leader of the Society in Pennsylvania. His grandson, William, father of Lieutenant John Claypoole, however, was the first to break away from the faith when he took to wife Elizabeth Hall, of the Episcopal church.

The name of David Chambers Claypoole has come down to us chiefly as a member of the firm of Dunlap and Claypoole, official printers of the Continental Congress. At their shop, 48 High Street, now 134 Market, the site of which is today marked by a bronze tablet, were first printed the Declaration of Independence, the Constitution of the United States, and Washington's farewell address. In this same printshop, after the war, the enterprising David conducted the *Pennsylvania Packet and Daily Advertiser*, the first daily newspaper published in America.

With Washington falling back and Howe's vastly superior force pressing forward to encircle the capital, the patriot cause was apparently toppling toward ruin following the defeat at Brandywine Creek. Each succeeding day seemed to bring more nerve-racking news than the one before to the city hemmed in by hostile cannon. Sixty-three young men of Mad Anthony Wayne's division, surprised by the enemy in a woods near Paoli, died by the bayonet, and wild rumors exaggerated the number to hundreds. Then came word that Howe, making a feint toward Reading, had suddenly swooped down upon Germantown, with Washington far up the Schuylkill powerless to prevent; and finally on the morning of September 26, the hair-raising news that Lord Cornwallis was actually advancing into the city!

Three excited farmers, flying ahead on horseback, brought word of his coming. From end to end of High Street they galloped, loudly calling their news. People on the sidewalks and at the market house stopped, listened, then raced for their homes or shops. Visions of sack and pillage and sharp bayonets still red from the blood of Paoli caused a further scramble of Whigs to get out of town. Many families fled without pausing to pack their household belongings. The river was full of rowboats hurrying to the Jersey shore. The horse ferry was pitifully inadequate for such a rush of business.

It was one of those sweltering days in late September which Philadelphians so often experience. But the heat stopped the frightened Whigs no more than it halted the invading host. Down the six-mile stretch from Germantown marched the British—past the fenced-in fields of ripening corn, the white farmhouses and country seats and orchards laden with apples. In the words of a Revolutionary historian:

Cornwallis came with a brilliant staff and escort, followed by splendid legions of British and Hessian grenadiers, long trains of artillery and squadrons of light dragoons, the finest in the army, all in their best array; stepping to the swelling music of "God Save the King," and presenting with their scarlet uniforms, their glittering arms and flaunting feathers, a striking contrast to the poor patriot troops who had recently passed through the same streets.

Swinging into Second Street from the Germantown road, with the German bands blaring their approach, the marching men crossed Arch Street scarce a hundred fifty yards from the home of Betsy Ross Ashburn. Few, if any, in that calm Quaker neighborhood had fled the city. Such was not their philosophy. Certainly it was not Betsy's. With what different emotions, however, from those which the parade of Washington's army had inspired, did this alert young woman now stand at the street corner surveying the incoming tide of redcoats! Astonishment undoubtedly and probably disdain at their gorgeous display—and apprehension for her beloved city as she gazed at the seemingly endless line of the conquerors. And

She Viewed with Astonishment the Seemingly Endless Line of
Cornwallis's Troops

this was only a part of General Howe's army, she was told. The commander himself, with most of his legions, was still in camp in Germantown.

On past the stately Christ Church went the red-coated soldiers; past the rows of shops whose doors had been hastily barred. In Second Street and Arch Street today there are many old houses still standing, from the windows of which timid citizens peered out that morning to see what manner of monsters the British really were—and their "Hessian hirelings."

Up in Boston, just a year before, the king's troops had seized Old South Church and turned it into a riding school for General Burgoyne's light dragoons. They had torn out the pulpit and pews, using some of the latter for fuel and some as pigsties. They had spread the floor of the sacred edifice with dirt and gravel and fixed a bar at the main doorway for the horses to leap at full speed. To excuse these things, they had spoken scoffingly of Old South as "a meeting house where sedition had been preached."

Now, as he rode down Second Street, the appraising glance of the British leader must have lingered eagerly on the massive pile of Old Christ

Church. But if so, he probably dismissed his thoughts, recalling what a hornet's nest had been stirred up by the desecration of Old South.

At Chestnut Street, Cornwallis turned west to the State House, where his officers took possession of the empty halls of Congress and bivouacked the main body of their troops in the spacious State House yard reaching back to Walnut Street, with artillery camped all about.

They looked up at an empty belfry, however. The precious Liberty Bell had been removed eight days before. Together with the chiming bells of Christ Church, it had been spirited out of the city, concealed amid the heavy baggage of a wagon train supposed to be carrying supplies to the American army. For a year it was to lay hidden beneath a church in Allentown, safe from the rapacious British bullet molders who sought everything in the way of metal.

The Tories were jubilant. This was their happy hour. Straightway they flocked to the State House with protestations of loyalty. Many who had swung to the rebel cause after Trenton and Princeton, now thought better of it and determined to stick to the king. Cornwallis and his staff were deluged with invitations to dine and wine.

First, however, they must find living quarters befitting their station. Very kindly the Loyalists guided them to the homes of wealthy patriots, who were thereupon politely but firmly dispossessed. Lord Cornwallis chose for himself the handsomely furnished house of Peter Reeve, a rich merchant, in Second Street near Spruce. The polished General Knyphausen and Count Donop, commanding the Hessians, took possession of a dwelling directly opposite. The talented and ill-fated Captain John André moved into Doctor Franklin's fine new home in a court opening on High Street above Third. For General Howe himself they reserved the mansion of former Governor Richard Penn, High Street below Sixth.

Meanwhile the soldiers, too, were making themselves at home. Grenadiers in their gorgeous coats of scarlet and cone-shaped service hats, strolled through High Street; florid-faced Teutons crowded the great room of the Indian Queen calling for beer and sauerkraut; squadrons of light horse galloped through country lanes and private roads scouting for forage and supplies.

12

The Gilded Ball and Weather Vane Provided a Fine Test of British Marksmanship. (One of the Interesting Exhibits Today in Carpenters' Hall is This Same Bullet-riddled Ball.)

New experiences indeed for staid old Philadelphia!

Carpenters' Hall, taken without ceremony from Samuel Griscom and his carpenter associates, now became a noisy rendezvous for his Majesty's dragoons. Revelry by night and musket practice by day jarred the nerves of near-by citizens. The gilded ball and weather vane atop the high cupola of the hall made an excellent target for troopers standing at the Chestnut Street end of Carpenters' Court, though their marksmanship was helped none too well by their frequent visits to the waterfront taverns.

Idleness, however, quickly came to an end among the troops under the rigorous discipline of Lord Charles Cornwallis. An administrator as well as a soldier was this young and active Britisher. The year he entered Philadelphia, he was thirty-nine years of age. The sight of one eye had been destroyed in his school days at Eton by a hockey stick, but he employed the other with double keenness. Of medium height, stockily built, with prominent nose and alert bearing, he proceeded to give the captured city a taste of the efficiency which made him, more than any other

British general, feared by the American commanders on the field of battle.

The townspeople saw him constantly in the
saddle, now directing the building of abatis along
Callowhill Street; now inspecting his troops on
parade; now organizing a census bureau to determine the city's population and resources.   Sir
William would soon be coming in, and everything
must be shipshape for him.

Day and night the streets echoed with the sound
of marching feet and the rumble of artillery wheels.
Companies of singing soldiers, engineers, and construction gangs filled Second and Third Streets on
their way to Callowhill, heedless of that quiet
Quaker section and its shocked sensibilities.
Washington might attack at any time from the
north, hence the hurrying line of earthworks.

And in the midst of these strange scenes, in the
seclusion of her upstairs rooms—she dared not
work now so close to the street—a young matron
with skilled fingers sewed, at every opportunity,
on flags for the ships and regiments of that leader
in whom rested all the American hopes.

All about her Arch Street dwelling, Elizabeth
Ashburn saw the finer homes of the Quakers shel-

tering British and German officers, whose brilliant uniforms and insolent bearing brought dismay a-plenty to the unwilling hosts. Her own house was probably too small to be considered by the invaders, and it is doubtful if they ever knew that rebel banners were being made above that innocent looking upholstery shop.

Only once, so far as is known, were redcoats inside her door. This was during the census-taking operation started by Lord Cornwallis. Groups of troopers were seen one day going from house to house in Arch Street. Two of them stepped within her shop. Smilingly they asked the number of persons in her household, their age and nationality. They asked her occupation, and then, glancing around at the chairs and sofas with their partly completed coverings, they quickly had their answer and went their way.

Cornwallis was particularly anxious to determine by the census the number of vacant houses available for Howe's quartermasters in the further billeting of British officers. He knew that many dwellings had been abandoned by the families of fleeing Whigs. The count, when completed, revealed 5,470 houses in the entire city, 587 of them

unoccupied. There were 287 stores. The total
population was found to be 21,767 inhabitants
exclusive of the army and strangers. This was
the first accurate census ever taken of Penn's
City on the Delaware.

XVI

Claypoole's First Fight

WITH Cornwallis in absolute control, Howe planning to enter soon with additional thousands, and the British battleships expected at any hour, the outlook could not have been blacker in the capital of the newborn nation.

Furthermore, General Burgoyne, the distracted people heard, was coming down from Canada with a superb British army to split the northern and central colonies apart.

The whereabouts of the statesmen who had so bravely signed the Declaration of Independence were now known to but few. Nobody knew what Washington was doing, though it was suspected that he was not idle. Tories were spreading reports that the war was over and that the rebel army would soon be disbanded.

Betsy Ashburn saw but little of her husband. All ships and galleys hugged the Jersey shore, the other side of Windmill Island which then stretched for a quarter of a mile along the middle of the river. The unarmed craft were ready to fly upstream should the hostile fleet be sighted. Rebel howitzers, floating about in the galleys and trained on the water front, constituted the only thorn in the side of the vigilant Cornwallis.

The days and nights were full of alarms. Even the Quaker community, in which Betsy lived, talked of little but the war and speculated on the fate in store for all.

It was hoped that Washington might launch some bold stroke like that at Trenton, and miraculously rescue the city from the invaders' grasp. There were rumors that he was planning just such a coup, and some of the more boastful predicted dire things for the enemy. But instead came the terrible affair at Germantown, which dashed the hopes of everyone. Betsy remembered it to her dying day.

A foggy night—the night of October 3. The roar of artillery toward the northwest just before dawn and the faint rattle of musketry. People roused from their slumbers, gathering excitedly in the streets. The fog so dense that the whale-oil lamps at the corners were obliterated ten feet away. Couriers racing into town to the British headquarters at Peter Reeve's.   Cornwallis at the head of his light horse thundering out Second Street immediately after.

Washington had attacked in the early morning, marching down from the Skippack valley by three roads.   He hoped to surprise and rout Howe's forces in the fog and then attend to Lord Cornwallis.   A well-laid plan, which the fog itself helped to defeat.

Germantown, now such a busy part of Philadelphia proper, was at that time a straggling village of small stone houses fronting on the one main highway, a half-dozen miles away.   Here and there a large mansion, the country home of some wealthy family.   Howe's army was encamped at the rears of the dwellings, in the fields and groves sloping down to the wooded Wissahickon Creek which flows into the Schuylkill.

Sir William was all unsuspecting of the attack. His outposts, driven back by the first onslaught, threw into a panic the regiments behind them. Greene and Sullivan, commanding the American left and right, pressed forward with a rush.   Mad Anthony Wayne was in the vanguard, thirsting to avenge Paoli.   A speedy victory was in sight, when a quick-witted British colonel, Musgrave, nipped it in the bud. He threw several companies of infantry into a large stone house, the beautiful home of Chief Justice Chew. From this fortress, they poured a withering fire which checked their attackers, covered the grassy lawn with dead and dying, and caused a fatal delay.

Howe's forces, retreating, now turned about and attacked. Elizabeth Ashburn's old suitor, John Claypoole, fighting under Greene, in this, his baptism of fire, found himself in a hand-to-hand conflict near the village market place. Surging masses of men were lunging wildly with their bayonets. All about him was a frightful din— shots, yells, curses, and cries of agony. In the fog and smoke he could scarcely tell friend from

From the Chew Mansion, the British Poured a Withering Fire

enemy. A deafening explosion near by hurled him to the ground. He struggled to his feet with difficulty, staggering from a sharp pain in his side.

He heard his comrades, with shouts of triumph, again driving the British back, when suddenly the fog, which had thus far helped them, played them a disastrous trick.

What happened is known to the reader of any history of the war. Mistaking a large body of Americans charging into the fray for British, Sullivan's men themselves retreated. Fearing they would be surrounded, they broke and ran. Greene's divisions, bewildered, also retreated. Then came the panic which turned an advance into wholesale flight, with Cornwallis and his cavalry, who arrived at that moment, pursuing the patriot army almost to the hills beyond Whitemarsh. Only Greene's masterly rear-guard action and Washington's cool-headed tactics saved it from rout.

Lieutenant Claypoole, escaping capture despite his wound, was carried along by his friends in Colonel Eyre's regiment. He was told that he had been struck by a flying fragment of a gun carriage in the melee near the market place. For a week he lay disabled with many others, in camp on the Perkiomen Creek, and to the end of his days the effects of his injury were to stay with him as a painful reminder of Germantown.

All day following the battle in the fog, the British, with their wounded and prisoners streamed into Philadelphia from the shot-riddled village. It was a very different kind of procession from those that had preceded it, which now filed slowly past the Quaker settlement at Second and Arch streets.   Howe and Cornwallis, riding together, halted at the State House, which they immediately put to a new and tragic use.

Doctor Rush's small city hospitals were totally inadequate for such an occasion—and the building from which liberty had been proclaimed was now called upon to house many of the victims of one of its bloodiest aftermaths.   Up the broad winding stairway to the second floor were carried wounded soldiers from the rough farm wagons which brought them in from the battle scene. Side by side they were laid in the great banquet hall running the full length of the building, British and Americans together—there to remain until they could be parceled out to private homes.

And thus the war in its cruelest aspects was brought to Philadelphia. It seemed that the entire population besieged the State House during these proceedings, struggling to learn the names of the injured or dead, watching the long procession of prisoners as it marched to the Walnut Street jail at the far end of the State House yard, and then turning to with a will to alleviate the suffering.

There was plenty to be done, especially by the womenfolk. For days and nights to come, Elizabeth Ashburn and her friends were busy making bandages, preparing nourishing broths, and visiting the State House and hospital wards, ministering to foe as well as friend. The Quakers, holding aloof from war, plunged with all their hearts into this work to help its victims.

Welcome indeed were these volunteer nurses wherever the injured soldiers lay. But they found a very different attitude at the provost prison, as the British termed the jail. For Provost Marshal Cunningham was in charge there and he admitted no kind-hearted visitors, only prisoners. Moreover, he had extraordinary ideas on the subject of rebel captives, his main object avowedly being to make them suffer for their crimes.

The reputation of "Hangman Cunningham," Howe's official jailor and executioner, had flown ahead of the British army in its travels. The man who freely boasted of the numbers of rebels he had done away with—who had hanged Nathan Hale after that awful battle on Long Island, refusing the young New Englander the services of a clergyman, and tearing to shreds the farewell letter he had written his mother, now became a sinister figure in Philadelphia. Those who watched him, thick-set, stoop-shouldered, as he daily sauntered through Sixth Street on the way from the prison to his chief's High Street residence, shuddered for the safety of those in his keeping. Well they might, for, in revenge for the affair at Germantown, he now outdid himself in cruelty.

From the miserable interior of the two-story stone prison, within a week, leaked tales which froze the blood of all who heard them. And every now and then a little group of red-coated guards was seen marching, heavily burdened, from the jail gates to the Potter's field, directly opposite, in what is now Washington Square. A convenient place to bury traitors to the king who died of punishment or disease—this Potter's field—and frequent use did Cunningham make of it.

XVII

The Captive City

BUT other events were to bring new terrors and supply Cunningham with more prisoners. The ensuing months indeed were like some dreadful and fantastic dream to the inhabitants of the captive city. A period of alarms and forebodings; of frightful battles at their very door; of business and financial failures; of despair for a starving army they depended upon to protect them, and of gaiety and excesses by their captors which threw into sharper relief their country's plight.

For Elizabeth Ashburn, parted from her husband; for her friends, the Claypooles, anxious over John and his wound, for everyone, in fact, except the Tory friends of the invaders, there were sleepless nights with but little to warrant an optimistic view.

Scarcely had the shock of the battle at Germantown died away, when the city was again shaken by rumors of coming combat. The British fleet was now in the lower Delaware, but could not sail up because of the two forts which guarded the river just below the city. Lord Howe determined to demolish them. General Washington was just as anxious to preserve them and decided to send strong reinforcements to the garrisons.

It was this decision which brought to Lieutenant John Claypoole his second ordeal of battle, which proved to be no less sanguinary than his first at Germantown. One night, shortly after he was on his feet again after that disastrous affair, he found himself, with many others, stealthily crossing the river in a fleet of rowboats. They were bound for Fort Mercer at Red Bank, on the Jersey shore, which derived its name from a steep gravel bluff rising from the water's edge. Their orders were to hold the fort at all costs against the coming attack.

They had not long to wait. General Howe had detailed the Hessians to capture Red Bank. Crossing from Philadelphia late in October, the German divisions, led by the handsome and dashing Count Donop, formed at Haddonfield, then marched against the fort across the farm lands abutting the river. An easy victory was expected over the little garrison commanded by Colonel Christopher Green of Rhode Island.

But they had not reckoned on the fierce defensive fight of which it was capable, and the ditches and abatis constructed about the walls. The first onslaught was met by a deadly fire which threw the Hessians into disorder and forced a quick retreat. Forming again, they rushed to the attack, and again were repulsed with heavy losses. Count Donop was mortally wounded. After an hour of bitter fighting, in which the Continental galleys did their part from the river, the Hessians withdrew as the sun was setting, leaving the cornfields about the fort strewn with dead and wounded, among them their fallen leader.

The garrison was beside itself with joy. At that moment, with the Stars and Stripes still flying overhead, they were the proudest troops in the whole Continental Army. And prouder still was Lieutenant Claypoole that evening when their gallant commander, Colonel Green, selected him as one of those to carry dispatches to General Washington, telling him of the victory.

In later years, when peace had returned to the land, of all his varied war experiences, Claypoole was fondest of telling his children of the victory at Red Bank, and of the perils of that journey.

13

Leaving his comrades as darkness fell, he picked his way among the slain Germans, was rowed to the Pennsylvania shore and, skirting the city to the westward, made his way to Washington's camp above Whitemarsh.

But the American triumph was short lived. Sir William Howe, blazing with wrath at the Hessian failure, ordered Lord Cornwallis himself to proceed against the rebel strongholds—to destroy them at any sacrifice. Once more the streets of the old city were filled with marching men as the flower of the British army, with their heaviest artillery, made ready for the assault. By flatboat and galley, they swarmed across the river, below the forts, while the townsfolk trembled in anticipation.

Those were anxious days for many households, particularly the homes of the defenders of the forts—and none suffered more than the parents and sisters of Lieutenant Claypoole. Word had reached them that he was at Fort Mercer, but, unfortunately for their peace of mind, they did not know that he had rejoined the main army. Betsy Ross Ashburn, alarmed over the safety of her own husband and ignorant of his whereabouts, was now almost constantly at the Claypoole home, consoling her friends and getting what comfort she could in return.

How they existed through that period of uncertainty they never knew. And when the bombardments finally came, rocking the solid brick dwellings day after day as though by an earthquake, lighting up the city with lurid glares by night, the frightfulness of war seemed beyond human power to endure.

From a line of shore batteries, Cornwallis poured a storm of shot and shell on the doomed forts, while the battleships did the same from below. British batteries on the Pennsylvania side contributed to the din. Caught between these fires, Fort Mifflin, on Mud Island, was demolished after heroic resistance, and Mercer fell a few days later. Commodore Hazelwood's fleet of galleys and armed brigs fought desperately, but the odds were too great and they were scattered upstream. It was not without bitter loss to themselves, however, that his Majesty's forces prevailed. The blood of many of Cornwallis's troops made redder still the soil of Red Bank; the British sloop of war, *Merlin*, ran aground and burned to the water's edge, while the fine new 64-gun frigate *Augusta* lay at the bottom of the river, blown up by a hot shot from a rebel cannon which sank deep into her vitals. The roar of that explosion and the shattering of glass all over town was an unforgettable climax of that reign of terror.

Sir William Howe and Lord Cornwallis now settled down to enjoy the comforts of city life after the discomforts of battle. The jail doors of Provost Marshal Cunningham had closed securely upon the survivors of the troublesome garrisons of the forts; communication with the sea was now unobstructed, and the Royal Navy rode peacefully at anchor in plain view off High and Chestnut streets. The line of abatis from river to river along Callowhill Street was nearing completion and would guard against attack from the north. Sir William's brother, Admiral Richard Howe, and his officers, moreover, were ready to be initiated by their army friends into the mysteries of shore life.

Besides this, "Mr. Washington," they understood, had retreated farther back into the hills and was having a hard time to hold his motley army together—even to find food and clothing—so why worry about him?

As the winter came on, Philadelphia became the gayest city in the colonies. Dinners and dances at General Howe's or the homes of wealthy Tories; plays at the old Southwark Theater, in South Street, directed by Captain André and Captain Delancy; tavern revels every night by soldiers and sailors; these gave sober-minded citizens much to ponder over as they went about their daily business, with prices of necessities soaring, commerce completely cut off, and many old Philadelphia firms going into bankruptcy.

All Continental ships and galleys at the port were now in hiding up the river and in the creeks and coves between Burlington and Trenton, ordered there by Washington to prevent their falling into the enemy's hands. Far up the winding Ancocas (now Rancocas), and the Neshaminy and Crosswicks creeks, many of the merchant vessels also took refuge. Betsy Ashburn's husband might have been in some foreign country for all that she saw or heard of him that fall and winter.

But she soon became thankful that he was safe and with a fair degree of comfort in his boat upstream, for with the snows of December, bad news began to make its way in from the hills of Valley

Forge and the patriot army they were all so anxious about—news which threatened to destroy their last remaining hopes for the cause. "Naked and starving" were the very words General Washington himself had used in conveying to Congress a picture of the plight of nearly a third of his troops. But Congress, at the remote village of York, with roads impassable, and out of touch with the various capitals, was either unable or unwilling to respond.

During that never-to-be-forgotten winter of 1777–78, Betsy's energetic fingers worked but little on flags. They were devoted to the desperate needs which occupied women of all classes in every street and alley of the Quaker City. To card, spin, and weave clothing and blankets; to gather together boots and shoes, medicines and foods, was part of the task; to smuggle them through the vigilant British patrols was another. But spurring those Revolutionary mothers constantly to superhuman efforts and ingenuity were their thoughts of the ragged regiments encamped on those bleak hillsides—men and mere boys, scores of whom they personally knew—weak from cold and hunger and disease—their shoeless, bleeding feet leaving crimson trails through the snow.

The daily sight of Sir William Howe, immaculately groomed, riding complacently about the streets in the luxurious coach of Israel and Mary Pemberton, and looking not unlike General Washington himself in face and stature, did not add to their peace of mind. This elaborate equipage, acknowledged to be the finest in the city, had quickly caught the eye of the British commander the day of his arrival, and he had promptly taken possession of it, with Friend Pemberton an exile in far-off Virginia, and his gentle wife powerless to prevent.

In January it was learned that Washington's eleven thousand followers had dwindled to less than six thousand able-bodied troops through death and illness. Sir William heard it too in the midst of his gay whirl. Victory could have been his for the taking, but instead of hurrying to Valley Forge, he decided to wait for spring and warm weather. Occasionally, one of his regiments made half-hearted sorties against the scouting rebel bands of Colonel Moylan or Captain Allen McLane who roamed the countryside. But they were gestures merely, which invariably came to naught.

It was in revenge for a more daring raid than usual by Captain McLane that the red-coated soldiers, returning one night from a futile pursuit, aroused the whole city to furious but helpless resentment by putting to the torch beautiful country seats along their path, which they termed "shelter lookouts for rebels." Flames from Fairhill and Sommerville, the stately homes of Isaac Norris and Charles Thomson on the Germantown road, lighted up the sky, and the following day it was discovered that Peale Hall and Jonathan Mifflin's house on the banks of the Schuylkill were also in ruins.

* * * * * *

And so the winter dragged on toward spring, and as the snows melted away, so did General Howe's chances. His golden opportunity was gone, for a rapid change had come to American fortunes.

While the susceptible Sir William was basking in the smiles of Tory maids and matrons, an alliance was being arranged between France and the United States by the sagacious Doctor Franklin who had gone to Paris, and a French army and fleet would soon be on their way across the ocean.

Furthermore, the British cause in the north had suffered a staggering blow at Saratoga with the surrender of General Burgoyne, who had invaded from Canada, and Washington's army, supplied with food, clothing, and reinforcements, had so far recovered from its winter hardships as to be once more a formidable fighting force.

That John Claypoole had managed to survive the privations which had laid low so many of his comrades, always seemed a miracle to that young man himself. Glad indeed was he to see those snowy hillsides changing to green and yellow under spring's gentle breezes. Germantown, Red Bank, and Valley Forge, crowded into his first six months of campaigning, had given him almost more than he had bargained for in war's cruelty, filth, and mental anguish. Many a night during the long winter, as the winds whistled and howled about that cluster of rude log huts which sheltered the patriot army, he lay awake wondering as to the fate of his parents and sisters so at the mercy of drunken soldiery all about their home. And doubtless, too, thoughts of Elizabeth Ashburn and her safety crowded many times into his head—though she was now Joe Ashburn's dutiful wife, and not for him to dream about with too great frequency.

Early in May, it was noised about that General Howe was in disfavor with the British government because of his frivolous and idle winter and was to be displaced by Sir Henry Clinton. Also that the British army had been ordered back to New York.

Wonderful news, which set the whole town talking in subdued excitement and, reaching Valley Forge, placed Washington and his staff keenly on the alert.

But, before they departed, the British officers decided to stage two farewell parties which should help to make their visit long remembered. One was designed to vindicate their long-idle battle fleet, and the other—a social affair—was planned to outdo anything before seen in the Quaker City or elsewhere in America.

On the seventh day of May, Admiral Howe dispatched a squadron from his fleet on a trip up the river to seek out and capture the more important Continental ships of war. They might be useful, he thought, to take along when the British forces set out for New York. But none were found.

Expecting such a move, General Washington had ordered Commodore Hazelwood to scuttle and sink all his fighting craft.

An angry lot were the British commanders, cheated of their prey, as they turned their prows downstream toward Philadelphia the following day. But they loosed their feelings and much of their gunpowder as they sailed along. Bordentown, Burlington, and other settlements were interesting targets for their guns, with the populace fleeing to the farm lands for safety.

And then, May 18, came the Mischianza, in which the British forgot all their disappointments! Neither the ebbing fortunes of war nor Sir William's disgrace could deter them from one final fling of stupendous proportions as a climax to their winter gaieties. In fact, they decided to give the affair in honor of their popular commander in chief as a testimonial of their regard and to speed him on his way across the sea.

It was because of its varied and spectacular character that they called the fête a "Mischianza," an Italian word meaning medley. And to act as master of ceremonies they chose their debonair and accomplished comrade, Captain

John André. Strange travesty of fate, that he who was thus selected to lead them in their merrymaking, was soon to be appointed their representative in a very different rôle, which led to dishonor and death in the valley of the Hudson!

The Mischianza began one afternoon in May with a great pageant on the Delaware. In a long line of gaily decorated barges, the hundreds of English and German officers with their Tory guests were carried slowly down the river, while Hessian bands boomed forth "Rule Britannia" and "God Save the King," and noisy salutes flared from the guns of the British warships, drawn up in a double line with all flags flying. At the fine old country mansion of Joseph Wharton, below the city, the company disembarked, and on the broad lawns of that deceased Quaker merchant, a tournament and tilting contest were held. "Knights of the Blended Rofe, armed with lances, fought Knights of the Burning Mountain for the favour of fair ladyes," according to a current account of the affair, "all being elaborately coftumed, the knights mounted on gray and black chargers richly caparifoned."

In the evening there was a huge banquet, at which Madeira and Burgundy went often around the tables, and the king's health and General Howe's were pledged so many times that the guests could not remember the number—nor anything else. Then followed a display of fireworks, and theatrical entertainments for which Captain André had painted the scenery, after which the knights and ladies danced in a ballroom in the Wharton house, especially built for the occasion, until four o'clock in the morning.

A colorful and edifying spectacle for Philadelphia's impoverished citizens! The Mischianza, widely heralded beforehand, drew crowds to the water front. As the river pageant floated by with the tide, and the revelers' songs rose high above the crash of the German cymbals, astonishment quickly changed to disgust and anger. Assembled on the bank beside their old meetinghouse at Front and Arch streets, near which Joseph Wharton lay buried, groups of Quakers looked on in silence. And what pained them the more was the knowledge that some of the wealthier members of their own Society were guests on the barges! Peggy Shippen, beautiful daughter of a family of Tory sympathies, and many other favorites of the dashing British officers contributed to the success of the occasion.

But this was the wind-up of the British frivolity and of their fruitless conquest of Philadelphia. Elizabeth Ashburn awoke one rainy morning, June 18, to discover that the army had marched out during the night, while the fleet had quietly weighed anchor, taking the families of many loyalists with it. To her astonishment and distress she was told that Pastor Duche, of Christ Church, was among them. His sympathies for the cause of independence, never very strong, had given way entirely during the British occupation.

Sir Henry Clinton and his fifteen thousand men had crossed to the Jerseys below the city, it was learned, and were hurrying toward New York by way of Haddonfield, Moorestown, and Mount Holly. For a distance of twelve miles, residents of those frightened Quaker settlements afterward related, the procession of baggage trains, horse, foot, and artillery stretched in a continuous line along the muddy highways.

A delirium of joy swept through the city at this sudden release from bondage. To Philadelphians it was a second declaration of independence. Flags, long hidden, reappeared at windows. Men crowded the taverns to celebrate. Pale, shrunken prisoners stepped from the dark cells of the provost's jail to the glorious light of day.

When that same night Captain Joseph Ashburn tied the *Swallow* up at her old mooring at the foot of Race Street, after her months of concealment up the river, and appeared in the doorway of his home, the perils of war were forgotten and forgiven in that little dwelling. General Washington, he brought word, had raced northward from Valley Forge at streak of dawn, had crossed the river at Coryell's ferry, and was hurrying to intercept the British column in northern Jersey.

Intercept it he did, but the bloody battle of Monmouth, thanks to General Lee's disobedience of orders, failed to stop the flying Clinton, who shook off his pursuers and marched into New York.

Congress now came back from its York refuge, the Liberty Bell mysteriously reappeared in the State House belfry, and patriot hopes ran high.

But in many households, particularly among the Quakers, these things were dwarfed by a still greater cause for rejoicing—the return of the Virginia exiles!

Moved by the beseeching letters of Mary Pemberton and Elizabeth Drinker, General Washington had ordered their release. And when, one evening a few days after the British had left, a little procession of stagecoaches rumbled into town and deposited the long-absent husbands and fathers at their homes, special meetings for prayer and thanksgiving were called in the Bank Meeting and the Great Meeting House in High Street.

To no one did the city's liberation come as a greater blessing than to Captain Ashburn and his wife. The former could sail again on his profitable voyages, and the latter could resume, unrestricted, her flag-making and upholstery business. The renewal of the double income meant much to their fortunes.

An event was soon to happen, moreover, which made this income all the more important. On the fifteenth of September, 1779, a baby daughter, Zilla, was born at the little house in Arch Street. This engrossing addition to Betsy's daily routine might have seriously interfered with the duties of her shop had it not been by now that she had helpers busily at work both on furniture coverings and sewing the bunting of red, white, and blue.

Steadily the Stars and Stripes had grown in use, for ships and for the army, until scarcely a week passed without bringing its orders for banners—most of them in purest wool and some in lustrous silk.

The days went quickly by. Betsy's husband was frequently at her side, and the war once more seemed a thing far removed.

Happy days they were! But only a brief interlude before the swift coming of events which were again to cast the dark shadow of tragedy over her home.

XVIII

Ashburn's Last Voyage

SOMEONE has defined adventure as "the misfortunes of a person in a far-off place." Apparently many of us deliberately seek misfortunes, if this be correct, and derive our greatest thrills in life from doing so.

It was possibly this singular trait of human nature that led Lieutenant John Claypoole, late of the Continental army, to cast his lot upon the sea. It may have been the example of his old friend, Captain Ashburn.

At any rate, these two young men, in the years 1780–81, met adventures in a far-off place which paled their previous war experiences and brought a strange and dramatic turn to the life of the maker of the first American Flag. How these events came about is recorded in a small memorandum book or journal kept by Claypoole on his wanderings, which has withstood the ravages of time and is now in the possession of descendants of Betsy Ross. One may explore in vain the realm of fic-

tion for a tale more romantic than that disclosed
in part by its pages.

Lieutenant Claypoole's old wound received at
Germantown proved a handicap to his military
ambitions. Though at first he had made light of it,
as time went on he found himself unable to stand
long marches over rough country. He therefore ten-
dered his resignation at the completion of his term
of enlistment, this decision being influenced also
by the illness and death of his father in the spring
of 1779 and solicitude for his mother and sisters.

Washington's army was at this time watching
that of Sir Henry Clinton in New York. Cornwallis was in the south with his famous cavalry
raider, Colonel Tarleton, overrunning the Caro-
linas, and Greene, Morgan, and Lafayette were
doing their best to keep them out of Virginia.
Things were looking blue again for the American
cause, and even the most optimistic were asking
how much longer the war was going to last.

Philadelphia, now ruled by Benedict Arnold,
whom Washington had appointed military governor, was given over to excesses and extrava-
gances, despite the serious outlook, almost as
great as those instituted by General Howe.

Arnold, the distinguished soldier, living in the High Street residence vacated by Sir William, entertained lavishly and sank deeply in debt while he paid court to the beautiful Peggy Shippen. Even members of the Congress and the Legislature were drawn into the giddy whirl following the British departure, bringing bitter complaints from General Washington that they should take his cause so lightly. And this was not all. With men like Franklin, Jefferson, and Adams away on important missions, he found disgraceful intrigues on foot to discredit his leadership.

John Claypoole was now twenty-eight years old and, notwithstanding his physical handicap, was full of the spirit and energy of youth. Viewing with disgust the excesses in the city's official life, he was anxious to get back into the service. Upon leaving the army, he had essayed to carry on the leather tanning business established by his father. But this was not to his liking. Of a studious nature, like his cousin, David Claypoole, editor of the *Daily Advertiser*, he devoted much of his time to writing. Many of his leisure hours he spent in his cousin's shop in High Street. But the war was in his blood and lured him to take part again in some branch of its excitement. He determined to try his luck on the sea.

Never much inclined to the water since the days when he and Joe Ashburn had sailed their catboat up to Burlington Island, or down the Delaware Bay after weakfish, he had given a ready ear recently to the tales his friends were telling of the thrilling life on a privateer. It was great fun dodging King George's fleet and perhaps picking up a prize or two in the form of a richly laden merchant ship flying the Union Jack and carrying luxuries to Sir Henry Clinton.

Long before the Revolution, there was an American merchant service. It grew so rapidly as to excite the jealousy of British merchants and shipowners. American sailors were noted for their skill and enterprise. In ships which today would look like toys, they made voyages which astonished the world—and this colonial merchant marine quickly became the navy of the newborn nation.

It was a large vessel in those days that exceeded a hundred feet in length. With crowded sails and straining spars, a skipper managed to cross the Atlantic in from four to six weeks—but only with favoring winds and smooth seas.

Nearly all trading vessels carried guns for protection against pirates—and by adding a few more guns to privately owned ships when the war came on, they became privateers. Unable to cope with the British ships of the line or with the larger enemy privateers, these nimble schooners and brigs were still of great service in bringing supplies and munitions for Washington's army and in harassing the king's commerce. Each captain was armed with letters of marque, giving him government authority to make prize of all ships and merchandise belonging to Great Britain.

After Sir Henry Clinton left Philadelphia, the shipping business bounded up again, and privateering attracted hundreds of adventurous youths. For many it also spelled disaster, for there were those who were as rash as they were brave. The British ships were swift and their gunners well trained. Moreover, angered by the failure of the king's armies to quell the rebellion, the Admiralty had given orders to sweep the seas clear of Americans.

The game, in fact, had now become so intense and the hazards so great that Joseph Ashburn, in the fall of 1780, decided to part company with the brig which had taken him on so many West

Indian voyages, and seek a larger and faster ship which could be more heavily armed. The *Swallow* was old and not in the best of condition. She had seen many years of buffeting. She was small, of but thirty tons register, and she had been acting badly in the gales which screamed up and down the coast and into Delaware Bay. Ashburn, urged by a prudent wife to make a change, was loath to risk another winter on her deck in combat either with the storms or the enemy.

Better for him, perhaps, had he not swapped horses, in the light of what happened, but neither he nor Betsy could read into the future.

When he was offered command of a new and larger craft then building on the stocks for the influential firm of McClenachan and Moore, he jumped at the chance. But the boat would not be launched until early spring, and he could not spend the winter in idleness. The British occupation had dealt a disastrous blow to Philadelphia shipowners, and there were more masters than vessels then at the port, even though the ship-wrights up above Race Street had been working day and night to replace the vessels that had been scattered and sunk.

In this emergency, Ashburn was urged by Messrs. McClenachan and Moore to take a temporary commission as first mate on the fine new brigantine *Patty*, then about to sail. The *Patty*, though not one of the largest boats of her class, was fleet and modern. She was built for short cruises—a square-rigger of fifty tons. She carried a crew of nineteen men, and on her decks, gleaming like gold in the Autumn sunlight as she lay at her wharf, were six new brass nine-pounders, which promised to give a good account of themselves in any adventure in which they might be needed. Besides this, she was commanded by one of Ashburn's old friends, Captain Francis Knox, whose persuasions that he sail with him settled the question. The *Patty* was to cruise to the West Indies, picking up any prizes that happened in her path, and Knox knew how familiar his friend was with every island in the group.

They weighed anchor one day early in October. Ashburn had bidden his wife and baby daughter an affectionate farewell and Betsy had walked arm in arm with him down Arch Street as was her wont, to wave a final good-by from the wharf as he dropped downstream. The Stars and

Stripes, made by her own hands, which the *Swallow* had flown from her spanker gaff, and now adorning the new brigantine, floated gaily in the breeze as the *Patty* swung out to take the current —and who shall attempt to describe the thrill of pride it gave her! "Betsy's flag," Ashburn always

The Stars and Stripes, Made by Her Own Hands, Floated Gaily in the Breeze

called the nation's new emblem, and so it was known among his men.

Ordinarily she looked for her husband's return from such expeditions in six weeks' time, and now, with a faster ship, she hoped it would be sooner. In fact, he had assured her he would beat his former time by many days, even allowing for the sport of chasing enemy merchantmen. But when November came and went without bringing him back, it did not give her worriment. Both he and Knox were skilful sailors; they knew every mile of the coast and their boat, she felt sure, could show a clean pair of heels to an enemy too powerful to attack.

When winter set in, however, with its heavy weather, it brought misgivings which turned to real anxiety by the end of the year. Every new storm, every reported fight at sea gave her fresh alarm. She scanned the war bulletins at the State House with their growing lists of names. She took to visiting each day the offices of McClenachan and Moore. They could give her no information. The river front, with its forest of masts and the great prows of ships stretching from their

They Could Give Her No Word of the Missing Brigantine

carved figureheads across the cobblestones almost to the warehouses opposite the docks, saw much of her that winter. She made inquiries of each incoming captain, and accosted the groups of seamen hanging about the Crooked Billet and the Coffee House, hoping to pick up some word of the missing brigantine. They could only shake their heads or attempt a cheery reassurance which she knew belied their true feelings. Several vessels, she learned, were long overdue. The British blockade was tightening. Large cruisers were lurking about the Delaware capes.

Each time a sail was sighted from the wharves, beating its way up the river or borne in on the flood of the tide, some friendly longshoreman or neighbor would quickly carry her the news. Hurrying then the two squares to the water front, she would stand shivering in the chill winds in a suspense of hope and fear until the craft's identity was revealed—only to retrace her steps with sinking heart.

February came, and with it the birth of another little girl, Eliza, on the twenty-fifth of the month. This tiny arrival slept on its mother's breast in placid ignorance of the anxiety that reigned within. Occupying herself with her children, Mrs. Ashburn tried to accept the consoling theories of her friends—that her husband was a prisoner of war and that his safe return was simply a matter of time. They were right in one particular, but none of them could foresee how fatally wrong in the other.

At this time, another sorrow added to her burdens. Her father, Samuel Griscom, with whom she had become reconciled as the years passed following her eviction from the Quaker faith, was now facing financial ruin. Building, crippled by the war, had entirely ceased when the British seized the city. What was worse, Cornwallis's men had confiscated the Griscom lumberyard at Fourth and Vine streets for the construction of their fortifications along Callowhill Street. Other trades had likewise suffered, and while incomes decreased, living expenses rose to unprecedented figures. In the distracted condition of the country, many families of means and position saw their fortunes swept away.

From their comfortable home in Arch Street below Fourth, Samuel and Rebecca Griscom moved to a small house adjoining their old lumberyard in Vine Street. Here they lived with dwindling income until 1793, when a final tragedy overwhelmed them. In that year, whose horrors to Philadelphians were scarcely second to those of the war, the great Yellow Fever Epidemic, made famous by Longfellow's "Evangeline," claimed them both among its hundreds of victims.

* * * * * *

Let us now see how John Claypoole fared on his maiden voyage. It was on the seventh of November, 1780, according to his journal, that he sailed down the Delaware. Unlike his friend, Joe Ashburn, he had shipped on a large transatlantic ship, almost a frigate in size, the privateer *Luzerne*, which was armed with eighteen sixpounders and was bound for Port L'Orient, on the west coast of France. An ambitious voyage for one just becoming acquainted with the sea! And a thrilling one as it turned out.

For seven weeks the *Luzerne* plowed through heavy seas, stormy days, and jet-black nights, losing one man overboard while battling with the gales, and reaching Port L'Orient January 1. She then discharged her cargo consisting of "275 hogſheads of tobacco and other articles and took in her homeward bound cargo conſiſting of ſalt and different kinds of merchandiſe." Continuing, Claypoole writes:

> *This L'Orient is about half the ſize of Phil*[a]*. It is a tolerable pleaſant city and the inhabitants in general ſeem to be a verry induſtrious people—and with all remarkably polite and civil to ſtrangers, eſpecially to Americans for whom they expreſs the greateſt affection. Since I have been here, I have had a ſevere fit of ſickness which has well nigh carry*[d] *me off the ſod. In the time of my illneſs I lodged at the home of a Mrs. Lazaneck who treated me with ſuch mother like tenderneſs that I ſhall never forget it. She has 3 daughters who are verry amiable women and were likewiſe verry kind to me, often ſitting for hours by my bedſide and endeavoring to teach me to ſpeak their language in which I begin now to make tolerable progreſs.*

The memorandum book in which Claypoole recorded his adventures is of a type often carried by sailors of that period. Bound in what was once a waterproof cover, it would conveniently go into a coat pocket or could have been easily concealed about his person. Though now somewhat torn and mutilated, there are seventy pages

"Fortune, That Fickle Jade, Threw a Privateer in Our Way"

remaining which are legible. They are devoted partly to a diary and verses, and partly to letters written on his travels. The letters, addressed to no one in particular, and with no chance of mailing, apparently were written as a form of journal.

It may be that Claypoole's illness and his French lessons at the hands of Mrs. Lazaneck's amiable daughters delayed the *Luzerne's* departure. On this point the book does not enlighten us. At any rate, it was late in March when she set sail homeward bound.

From the hospitable docks of Port L'Orient to their own Philadelphia seemed but a matter of a few weeks to the captain and crew. A very different destination awaited them, however, and one which every American skipper at that time sought most to avoid. But let Claypoole's journal tell it:

Lenox, Cove of Corke
May 9th, 1781

. . . We set sail from L'Orient on the twenty-sixth of March in company with 7 sail, among which was the Lyon and the Ann, etc. We had a glorious breeze which lasted us for 7 or 8 days, about which time the Lyon parted with us and shap^d her course for the West Indies.

On the 4th of April as we were pleafantly failing and pleafing ourfelves with the profpect of foon being at home, all hands being in high fpirits having each of us a good venture on board, fortune, that fickle jade, threw a Privateer in our way who foon made a prize of us and with us fhap^d her courfe for Ireland. She was called the enterprife, commanded by a Thomas Eden and mounted 32 guns.

She got safe into Ireland with her prize in company, and came to anchor in the River Shannon about 10 miles up. A number of our crew fuch as chofe enter^d on board of her, the reft of us, 37 in number, were fent under guard and in irons (except 4, amongft which number was your humble fervt.) to the town of Limerick, where we were clofe confined in a fort of coach houfe in the Barrack yard and allow^d fixpence a day to fubfift on. . . .

Claypoole then describes the hardships of himself and his fellow captives in a march of seventy-two miles across country from Limerick to the Cove of Corke. There, after spurning repeated efforts to enlist them in the king's service, they were placed in irons on the prison ship *Lenox,* a frigate with seventy-four guns, wondering what would be their next disposition by his Majesty's government.

For six weeks they were confined in the dark hold of the ship, and then they knew.

XIX

Old Mill Prison

ON a rocky promontory jutting into the sea near the town of Plymouth, England, a quadrangular group of low stone buildings stood at the time of the American Revolution. The windows were small and heavily barred. The buildings were so arranged that, with high stone walls connecting them, they inclosed two large yards in which sentries with loaded muskets were

SINCE THE TIME OF QUEEN ANNE, CRIMINALS HAD BEEN HOUSED IN OLD MILL PRISON

15

(205)

stationed day and night.   In the tops of the walls were embedded broken glass bottles to make it more difficult to climb over.

This was the Old Mill Prison—famous or infamous among Yankee sailormen who made so bold as to resist the power of Great Britain on the seas.   Since the time of good Queen Anne, criminals had been housed there, the prison taking its name from an ancient windmill which originally marked the site.   A lonely place it was by day or night, a bleak, desolate stretch of headland, lashed by the sea and exposed to fierce wintry storms.   Among the fishermen and the country folk round about in the county of Devonshire, for over two centuries it had been food for strange tales and superstitious dread.

When King George's warships and privateers began to halt and make prizes of American merchantmen, the British convicts were removed to inland jails, and this old stone fortress on the southeast coast was one of those chosen to receive his Majesty's enemies taken on the high seas.

And by a grim irony of fate, indeed, was this selection made.   Plymouth!   A name endeared to New Englanders as the last port touched by the Pilgrim Fathers on their way to America in the *Mayflower*, and from which Plymouth Rock was named, was now to be cursed by many a New Englander who surrendered his liberty within the gloomy walls of Old Mill Prison.

A busy port Plymouth soon became, as the guard ships came in with their captives. All who could be impressed into service on British vessels escaped imprisonment. All who scorned the threats of their captors were charged with high treason and disappeared within the gates of Old Mill, not to come forth again until the end of the war, unless by an infrequent exchange of prisoners or unless, perchance, death set them free in the meantime.

And from the accounts of American patriots who languished there, death was a welcome relief to many. In the English jails of those days, there were no separate cells. Men of all classes were herded together. Neglect and ill treatment, common among ordinary convicts, were intensified with the "rebels" at Plymouth. Smallpox and other epidemics carried off scores. Many were shot trying to escape. All were debarred pens, ink, and paper, and newspapers, though these were occasionally smuggled in.

A diary written by Charles Herbert, of Newbury-port, Massachusetts, who was confined four years in Mill Prison, has contributed to its annals. He wrote in it from day to day, and concealed it under the false bottom of a chest.

"If prisoners try to escape or commit any minor offense," says this chronicle, "they are taken to the 'Black Hole,' a place of punishment so-called, where they lie 40 days on half allowance, and nothing to sleep on but the ground. Often the Black Hole is full, so many prisoners attempt to escape. The rations are so small that many are strongly tempted to pick up grass in the yard and eat it, and some pick up old bones that have been lying in the dirt a week or more and pound them to pieces and suck them. Often the cooks, after they have picked over our cabbage, will cut off some of the butt ends of the stalks and throw them over the gate into our yard, and I have often seen, after a heavy rain, when the mud would be over our shoes, the men running from all parts of the yard, regardless of the mud, to catch the butt ends of the stalks and nearly trample one another under feet to get a piece."

To the tender mercies of Old Mill Prison, John

Claypoole, of the privateer *Luzerne*, was consigned early in July, 1781. He records the event as follows:

Mill Prifon the 1ft of
Septr. 1781.

Sir,

The laft letter I wrote you was from on board the prifonfhip Lenox in the Cove of Cork, which Ship had orders to weigh Anchor which fhe did on the 21ft of June and fet fail for England in company with a fleet of near an hundred Sail, confifting of men of war, Frigates, Sloops of war, Tranfports merchantment etc. etc. On the 25th of June caft anchor in Plymouth found and on the 29th we prifoners were removed to a Guard fhip call^d the Dunkirk laying in Harbor where we rêmain^d till the 6th of July when myfelf with 9 others were carry^d before a Juftice of the Peace who after having examined us one by one in a verry formal manner told us that we ftood charg^d with High Treafon being found in arms and in open rebellion againft his King upon the high feas, for which crime, as he termed it, we were to be committed to Old Mill Prifon, there to remain till his King fhould be gracioufly pleafed to call our Tryal. Accordingly our mittemus'es were wrote and we were brought to this place where we have been now about 2 months and for aught I know fhall be here 2 years, for I do not fee any likly hood of our being exchanged, and it feems impoffible to get out of this place without the wretched alternative of entering into their Infernal service which however I find many are reduced to the neceßity of doing rather than ftay to fpend all their youthful days in this hatefull confinement.

There are about 300 of us here and our number is daily increafing, the Provifion we get here is ¾ of a pound of beef and a pound of coarfe bread p^r day which however fmall we make fhift to live on with the affiftance of fix pence a week which we are fupply^d from our own country.

This prifon is fituated on the fide of a Hill fo that we can fee a good diftance to fea, the prifon yard is about 70 or 80 yards fquare which ferves us to walk in and many a Solitary hour do we faunter away in it.

There is a number of printed rules hung up in the prifon where we are to regulate our conduct and the punifhment inflicted on us in cafe of Tranfgreffion is forty days confinement in the black hole upon half allowance, notwithftanding which we verry often attempt to make our efcape but there is fo ftrict a guard kept over us that verry few effect it. We have fent feveral petitions to the King of France, fetting forth in moving terms our deplorable fituation, humbly praying his moft Chriftian Majefty to fall upon fome method to get us reliev^d, but I fear the Britifh parliament are fuch a ftiff-necked fet of beings that they will not confent to let us go.

Yours etc. etc.

Jno. Claypoole

Had Claypoole but known it, it was through the efforts of his fellow townsman, the omniscient Doctor Franklin, then Minister to France, that the prisoners were supplied with the "fixpence a week." He interested himself in their behalf, protested to the British government against their ill treatment, and sought to have a shilling a week sent to each to purchase comforts. But it was difficult to obtain the funds. The shilling dwindled to sixpence, and often to nothing at all.

In addition to Herbert and Claypoole, Andrew Sherburne, of Portsmouth, New Hampshire, has left for Revolutionary archives an account of his experience in the fortress at Plymouth. "There had been practically no releafe or exchange of prifoners from Mill Prifon fince the commencement of hoftilities," he wrote. "Confequently fome had been there nearly feven years. At different times, numbers had efcaped and fome had fhipped on board his majefty's fhips, and thereby were abfolved from the heinous crimes of rebellion, piracy, etc. On one occafion, about a dozen prifoners made their efcape. They by fome means got out one of the grates of a window directly over the weft end door of the long prifon. They took a loofe beam and ran it out of the window in an oblique direction fo as to juft reach over the north wall of the yard. They lafhed hammocks together, fufpended them from the end of the beam and lowered themfelves down. Other prifoners carefully replaced the beam and the grating fo the guards would not detect the efcape.

"Whenever more Americans arrived, as they approached the inner gate, we would hear the cry, 'more prifoners,' 'more prifoners!' The inner gate was then opened, being well guarded by foldiers with fixed bayonets. The other prifoners would then rufh from all directions to the gate to fee if any of their acquaintances were to be found among the newcomers."

One day not long after his incarceration, John Claypoole was attracted by such a commotion as that described by Sherburne. He hurried to the gate, for the unvarying monotony of their lives made this a thrilling event to all.

As the line of arrivals filed through, he scrutinized each face. All were strangers to him except one. And that one gave him the surprise of his life. Unshaven, with disordered hair and clothing, he walked with halting step near the end of the procession.

Claypoole looked and looked again. He could not believe his eyes. Then he stepped forward.

"Joe Ashburn!"

The newcomer straightened up in astonishment.

"John Claypoole!" he returned. "How in Heaven's name did you get here?"

We need not dwell upon this strange meeting of the two old friends. That it seemed a miracle to both can well be imagined. Claypoole's journal does not record the story Ashburn told him of his wanderings. And the latter apparently kept no chronicle of his own. From October until July, he had presumably been on the sea, for a brief period in the brigantine *Patty*, and for a longer in British custody. Months frequently elapsed between the capture of Americans and their transfer to prison ships, and months more before they reached port. They were confined between decks—captains, lieutenants and crews, and often negro slaves—sleeping side by side on the floor and subsisting on salt provisions, while constant threats that they were to be hanged for treason added to their mental torment.

It was a very different figure from the doughty skipper he was accustomed to see striding along Arch Street or High Street, Philadelphia, that John Claypoole now welcomed among the guests of Old Mill Prison. Ashburn's ship was lost—his companions (there is no record of them) either slain or, like himself, made captive—his wife knew not where he was; his health seemed broken. He had not heard that Claypoole had enlisted on the sea, hence his surprise at finding him there.

Their old bonds of friendship now drew these two closely together in adversity. What long and intimate talks they must have had! What reminiscences of early days! What carefully guarded plans to escape! But the risks of death at the hands of the sentinels were great, and even if once outside the walls the chances were slim—so if they made such plans they did not attempt them. Only by plunging into the sea and swimming or by making one's way back along the bare and guarded headland, could one hope for freedom— and the dwindling strength of both made such an effort hopeless.

Moreover, the war news which trickled in from time to time, led them, despite the ridicule of their guards, to believe American victory was at hand. They had heard of successes both in the North and the South. They heard that Lord Cornwallis was being penned up in Yorktown by Washington's army, and the French fleet under Count de Grasse. Then on the twenty-fifth of November, five weeks after the event actually happened, word of the British surrender reached the prisoners, according to an entry in Claypoole's journal.

Sherburne states that it was a newspaper concealed in a loaf of bread that brought them the news. A sudden outburst of cheers amazed the guards. Hats and coats went aloft and epithets aimed at the king flew about the yard.

"A confiderable number furnifhed themfelves with the American enfign painted on a half fheet of paper, with the Englifh enfign painted below the Union," writes Sherburne, "and fticking this half fheet into their hat bands, paraded the yard, huzzaing in fuch a manner as to alarm the guard. The whole guard came into the yard, and fome of the prifoners had the hardihood to infult the guard and dare them to fire upon them. But by the interpofition of fome of the American officers, the tumult fubfided without any mifchief."

What part our two Philadelphians played in that celebration and in preparing the sketches of the Stars and Stripes, is not recounted. But of one thing we can be reasonably sure—they were thoroughly well acquainted with the design of the emblem and lacked nothing of fervor in flaunting it.

The surrender of Cornwallis and the prison celebration must have inspired the following triumphant bit of verse written in the little book of John Claypoole. Whether he or one of his fellow prisoners was the author is not stated.

An American Anthem

Let Tyrants ſhake their Iron Rod
and Slavery clank her galling chains,
we fear them not, we truſt in God
New England's God forever Reigns.

Howe and Burgoyne and Clinton too
with Preſcot and Cornwallis join^d
together Plot our overthrow
in one infernal League combin^d.

When God inſpir^d us for the fight
their ranks were broke their lines
were Fors^d
their ſhips were ſcatter^d in our ſight
or ſwiftly driven from our Coaſt.

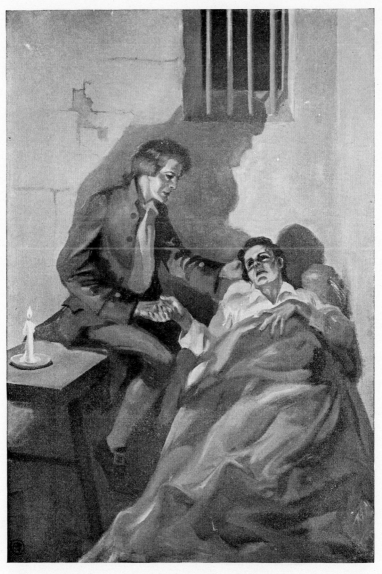

"In the Night of the 3d of March, Mr. Joseph Ashburn Departed This Life"

The Foe comes on with haughty ſtride
our troops advance with martial noiſe
their vetterans fly before our youth
and Generals yield to beardleſs Boys.

What grateful offerings ſhould we bring
What ſhall we render to the Lord
Loud Hallelujahs let us Sing
And praiſe his Name on Every Chord.

Thus the victory at Yorktown in far-off America, which made certain their country's freedom, brought renewed hope of speedy release to the wretched inmates of Old Mill Prison.

For many of them, however, there was to be no release, except to be carried in rough pine boxes to the burial ground a short distance outside the gates. A full year elapsed before peace was signed. And every week of that year seemed an eternity to the captives, with their jailers, who resented the turn of events, more brutal than ever, and epidemics filling the crude prison hospital.

To one of these maladies, Joseph Ashburn fell a victim as the winter of 1781–82 was nearing its end.

The robust mariner, used to the wild free life of the sea and taking its hardest knocks as they came to him, failed rapidly under prison confinement, while his friend, Claypoole, frailer of physique and weakened by an old wound, was among those, strange to say, who survived its torments.

Of the circumstances of Ashburn's illness and death we know little except the record left by his comrade. That record, brief as it is, and couched in the simple and homely language of the frayed journal, calls up a picture of tragedy and suffering which we must count it a blessing of Providence that the captain's young wife, three thousand miles away, knew nothing of at the time.

There are two entries, the first in the diary portion of the book:

In the night of the 3d of March (1782) Mr. Jofeph Ashburn departed this life after an illnefs of about a week which he bore with amazing fortitude and refignation.

And then the following in letter form:

Mill Prifon, May 20th, 1782.
My much loved Friend:
By the date hereof you will perceive that I ftill continue in this Dreary Manfion and will I doubt not think it a matter of furprife that I am not releasᵈ in fo long a time.

Indeed I am unable to account for the great delay that has been made in forwarding an exchange of prisoners as the brittish Parliament has 3 months ago passed an act for that purpose; ever since which time I have been in daily expectation of being releas[d] and which was the reason why I omited writing to you. But least you should be uneasy for my welfare, I embrace this opportunity of letting you know that I still continue to enjoy my health, which I think considering my situation is a little to be wondered at.

Our number is increased to near seven hundred and we are so much crowded that it begins to grow verry uncomfortable.

As I believe you were acquainted with Mr. Joseph Ashburn, I beg leave to inform you that he was brought to this prison a short time after us. He died in the night of the 3d of March after illness of about 10 days which he bore with amazing fortitude retaining his sences till the last moment of his life.

. . . It is a common practice with these rascals if any of us attempt to escape to fire on us and down with us at once. But notwithstanding all their vigilance a few make shift to get away sometimes. It is about 2 months since our friends Capt. Jn[o] Kemp and Allex Tindal with five others got off and as I am since inform[d] are safe arrived in France.

Your real friend and verry Humble Serv[t].

Jn[o]. Claypoole.

XX

Claypoole's Return

FOUR months after the body of Captain Ashburn was laid in an unnamed grave on that barren promontory on England's seacoast, the gates of Old Mill Prison were opened to set at liberty his friend John Claypoole.

The war was almost at an end. Prisoners were being exchanged. Claypoole and two hundred fifteen fellow captives were placed on board the cartel ship (exchange ship) *Symmetry*, at Plymouth, June 22, 1782. Fifty days later they sighted the Cape of Henlopen, and soon the young Philadelphian who had started out so blithely on his maiden voyage nearly two years before, was once more treading the streets of his native city.

He had two immediate missions in view. To one—the reunion with his family—he looked forward with intense eagerness. The other he counted the hardest task he had ever faced in his life.

His widowed mother and sisters, Susannah, Martha, and Clarissa, were overwhelmed with joy and astonishment at sight of him. They had long since given him up for lost. As in the cases of Ashburn and so many others, there had been no news to give them hope that he had survived the dangers that beset Revolutionary sailors.

It quickly got abroad among the neighbors that he had brought back some tidings of the missing captain, they knew not what, and though he lost no time in hastening from his home to that of Elizabeth Ashburn, he found the rumors there ahead of him. She was awaiting his coming in a fever of mingled hope and dread.

In the little sitting room at the rear of the upholstery and flag-making shop, she heard the news which was so difficult for him to reveal. Outside, in the garden, her three-year-old daughter, Zilla, was playing; while in a cradle slept the baby girl whom the missing father had never seen.

"Please tell me everything," said Mrs. Ashburn. He related the details as best he could remember them, stressing her husband's bravery to the end and his final messages to her. Nor did he attempt to check the tears which flowed down the cheeks of his listener. Her ceaseless anxiety

16

Mill Prison May 20th 1782
my much loved friend

By the date hereof you
will perceive that I still continue
in this Dreary Mansion. and
will I doubt not think it a
matter of surprize that I am not
releas; in so long a time.
Indeed I am unable to account
for the great delay that has been
made in forwarding an exchange
of prisoners as the brittish Parlia
ment has 3 months ago pased
an act for that purpose
ever since which time I have been
in daily expectation of being re
leas;   and which was the reason
why I omited writing to you.

But least you should be uneasy
for my wellfare,   I embrace

THE JOURNAL OF JOHN CLAYPOOLE WAS ONE OF THE MOST TREASURED
RELICS HANDED DOWN TO HER CHILDREN BY BETSY ROSS. MANY OF
ITS PAGES WERE IN THE FORM OF LETTERS WHICH HE KNEW COULD
NOT BE MAILED. APPARENTLY HE SOUGHT SOLACE IN CAPTIVITY BY
THUS IMAGINING HE WAS IN COMMUNICATION WITH THE OUTER WORLD,

This opportunity of leting you know that I still continue to en joy my health, which I think considering my situation is a little to be wonderd, at,

our number is encreased to near seven hundred and we are so much crouded that it begins to grow verry uncomfortable.

As I believe you were aquain ted with Mr Joseph Ashburn, I beg leave to inform you that he was brought to this prison in a short time after me, he died in the night of the 3d of March after an illness of about 10 days which he bore with amazing fortitude retaining his sences till the last moment of his life.

of the past twenty months now found relief in unrestrained emotion.

Her sorrow, however, did not make her oblivious of the well-being of her caller. Remembering his old wound, she was tenderly solicitous of the effects of his prison hardships upon his health. That his life at Old Mill Prison had taken its toll was evident in his face and manner. During those long and anxious months, Betsy had done much to console his grieving mother and sisters, even while enduring her own trial, and she rejoiced for their sakes to know that he was safe.

For some weeks following his return, John Claypoole was glad to remain in idleness in and about his home, recuperating from his experiences and resuming acquaintance with his friends. It was but a short walk around to Elizabeth Ashburn's, and whether from a mutual bond of sympathy or from an old longing recently revived, he found himself strolling frequently in that direction. To the oft-repeated story of her husband's last days in his company, the captain's widow did not tire of listening, and she in her turn told Claypoole of the happenings in America during his absence. She told him of Arnold's treason, following soon

HE TOLD HER OF HER HUSBAND'S BRAVERY TO THE END

after his marriage to Peggy Shippen; of his flight to the enemy; of the capture and sad death of Captain André, who had been promoted to the rank of Major, and plotted with him for the seizure of West Point. She described the excitement in Philadelphia when couriers brought the news of Cornwallis's surrender, the acclaim to Washington and his victorious troops when they returned from Yorktown on their way to New York, and the talk of the coming peace treaty. She told him how Robert Morris had saved the nation from bankruptcy the year before when he had borrowed an immense sum from France and pledged his fortune as security.

Most of Claypoole's old friends were still away with the army or on the sea, and in October the urge toward activity sent him off on another cruise. He shipped on board the *Hyder Ally*, which however fared better than his old ship, the *Luzerne*, and brought him safely back to Philadelphia near the end of the year.

On this voyage, with plenty of time for meditation under starlit skies, he evidently made up his mind on a highly important course of action. Upon his return, we find him calling more

frequently than before at the little Arch Street
house. The dictates of his heart, for so many
years subdued, were now openly avowed, and he
determinedly pressed his suit for the hand of the
lady who resided there.

And who will criticize him?

At thirty, Betsy Ashburn was as attractive as
at twenty, and with a new dignity and grace which
added to the subjugation of her old wooer. To
him she was very little changed from the girlhood
days when he used to watch her on her way to the
old Bank Meeting at Front and Arch streets, her
pretty face hidden under her broad-brimmed
Quaker bonnet.

We know not what her immediate answers were
to these new attentions, but we do know that on
the eighth of May, 1783, Elizabeth Ashburn was
joined in matrimony to John Claypoole. It has
also come down to us that one condition of her
consent was that the said John Claypoole should
give up once and for all his seafaring career. She
was resolved that he should not risk his life and
her happiness again in the fascinating though dangerous tilts with "Davy Jones" and King George.

XXI

The Fighting Quakers

BUT little more remains to be told. John and Elizabeth Claypoole, according to the first city directories published in Philadelphia, lived for several years after their marriage at the little brick house in Arch Street. Then they moved to a larger home in Second Street because of their growing family—and later to South Front Street.

Five daughters were born to them, Clarissa Sidney, Susannah, Rachel, Jane, and Harriet. The first two they named for John's sisters, whose friendship had meant so much to Betsy in the tragic years of the war. Harriet died in infancy.

Together, John and his wife conducted their flag and upholstery business. Later on, he accepted a lucrative position with the United States Custom House in Philadelphia, leaving to the capable Betsy the direction of their shop.

On Sundays, he went with her to worship at the meetings of the newly formed Society of Free Quakers, of which she was an original member.

(227)

The organization and early history of these "Fighting Quakers" constitutes one of the most interesting chapters in the career of this famous daughter of the Revolution.

Upwards of four hundred members of the Society of Friends were disowned during the war. Practically all owed their expulsion to direct or indirect participation in the conflict. At first they scattered to other churches, but as time went on some of the leaders in thought who clung to Quaker doctrines and modes of worship began to hold small group meetings at their various homes.

Samuel Wetherill, formerly a prominent minister at the Bank Meeting which Betsy Griscom had attended in her girlhood, was the prime mover. He was one of those who in 1777 had taken the oath of allegiance required by the Pennsylvania legislature, thus violating the Quaker testimonies. Moreover, his cloth factory had supplied Washington's troops at Valley Forge with material for uniforms. Other leading spirits were Timothy Matlack, disowned because he was a member of the Committee of Safety; Colonel Clement Biddle, quartermaster for General Gates at Valley Forge, and Peter Thomson, printer of the Continental money. Conspicuous among the women joining the group, was Lydia Darragh, a young matron who, in 1777, had warned the patriot army of a surprise attack planned by the enemy. Overhearing British officers, who occupied her house, discussing late one night a sortie upon Washington's forces encamped at Whitemarsh, she quietly left the house early in the morning and made her way through the lines disguised as a market woman. Cornwallis thus found Washington fully prepared and his plan came to naught.

During Captain Ashburn's long absence on the voyage which resulted in his imprisonment and death, his wife was drawn into this group of disowned Quakers. In her worriment and solitude, she readily accepted their invitation to seek comfort in the religious faith of her childhood, so long as it did not include the precepts on war and marriage to which she was so bitterly opposed.

In 1781, the Free Quakers drew up a constitution or discipline. There was to be no creed or testimonies or heresies. None who believed in God was to be disowned for any cause whatever. Military service in defensive war and marriage with persons of other religious denominations were expressly permitted.　In the course of their discipline they said:

> We acknowledge the kindnefs of Providence in awakening us to a view of the deplorable fituation in which we have been.　Difowned and rejected by thofe among whom we have been educated, and fcattered abroad as if we had been aliens in a ftrange land, the profpect of our fituation has indeed humbled us.　But he whofe mercy endureth forever, has preferved us and induced us to confide that he will care for us.　And being made fenfible of the indifpenfable neceflity of uniting together, we have caft our care upon the great preferver of men, and depending upon him for fupport, conceive it to be a duty which we owe to ourfelves, our children and families to eftablifh and fupport among us public meetings for religious worfhip. . . .

In 1783, the membership of the Free Quakers had so increased that it was decided to build a meeting house.　A plot of ground was purchased at the southwest corner of Fifth and Arch Streets, opposite the burial ground of Christ Church. Subscriptions were invited to the building fund and many outside the society contributed, among them General Washington and Benjamin Franklin.

The building, of simple design, was of substantial brick construction and still stands as one of the interesting landmarks of old Philadelphia. It was completed in the spring of 1784 and the first meeting within its walls was held June 13 of that year.

A marble tablet, built into the gable end fronting on Arch Street, has this interesting inscription:

By General Subscription
FOR THE
FREE QUAKERS
Erected in the YEAR
of OUR LORD 1783,
of the EMPIRE 8.

The last line on this tablet is one of the few permanent records of the belief then largely prevailing that the United States was to become an empire. Not until the Federal Convention met three years later and framed the Constitution of the Republic, did this idea disappear.

For a time after the completion of their meeting house, the Society of Free Quakers flourished and gained members rapidly. At one period the number was approximately three hundred. The old minute books and epistles are still in existence—

also a membership book compiled soon after the Society moved into its meeting house. It shows the bold signature of John Claypoole and the small delicate one of his wife, Elizabeth Claypoole.

The life of this couple was a happy one together for a period of perhaps fifteen years, at the end of which time the husband's health failed and he became a confirmed invalid. The injury at the Battle of Germantown, followed by the hardships of his prison life, had undermined his vigorous constitution—and, in middle age, he suffered a stroke of paralysis which left him a cripple to the end of his days. He died in 1817.

Meanwhile, Elizabeth Claypoole, whose robust health and buoyant nature seemed proof against all misfortunes, was busy rearing her family of

THE MEETING HOUSE OF THE FREE QUAKERS AT FIFTH AND ARCH STREETS, A SHORT WALK FROM THE HOME OF BETSY ROSS. HERE THE FLAG MAKER AND OTHER DISOWNED QUAKERS MET FOR WORSHIP.

daughters, taking care of her invalid husband, and managing her business. Five of the daughters grew to maturity, including Eliza Ashburn. The latter's sister, Zilla, died in her youth.

When Clarissa Sidney Claypoole, John's oldest daughter, became of age, she took an active interest in the flag-making business. She was married soon afterward to Jacob Wilson, and lived in Baltimore, but following his death, she returned to her parents' home and continued the manufacture of flags long after her mother gave it up. Margaret Boggs, a niece of Mrs. Claypoole, was also active in the business, which flourished until 1857.

Their customers were numbered by the score—shipping firms, merchants, and military organizations. Conspicuous among them was Stephen Girard, the wealthy Philadelphia shipowner and financier of the War of 1812. An interesting relic dating from early in the century and still in existence is a receipted bill, signed by Elizabeth Claypoole, for bunting for his trading vessels.

Betsy Ross Claypoole was the last survivor of the original group which established the Society of the Free Quakers. Samuel Wetherill, whose keen mind and ability as a speaker maintained him as its "clerk" or presiding officer until 1808, died in his eighty-first year, in 1816. Timothy Matlack and Clement Biddle soon followed him.

As political differences disappeared and the war became a thing of the past, the younger membership of the new society fell away. Many of the disowned Revolutionary soldiers, after the necessary apologies to their former meetings, were reinstated with the regular Friends. To the last, however, the maker of the first American Flag remained steadfast to the Free Quaker principles, though her daughters did not. In the year 1834 the society had dwindled to but two members, Elizabeth Claypoole and John Price Wetherill, grandson of its first leader. For weeks these two continued to meet for worship, sitting silently in the ministers' gallery facing the empty benches.

It is related that one day, as the meeting closed, John Wetherill said: "Widow Claypoole, there are but two of us remaining. It is not right that thee and I should continue to meet here alone." Whereupon he locked the door with the huge old-fashioned key and they went their ways.

Thus the Free Quakers, as a religious society, passed out of existence. But to this day it con-

The great End for which it pleaseth the Almighty to bring Mankind into Existence, is, that they may faithfully serve him here on Earth, and glorify him for ever hereafter. He in his infinite Goodness, is constantly calling upon them to come and learn of him, who is Wisdom itself; and We doubt not, but that those who adhere to his divine Instruction will be rewarded with everlasting Peace; and for his manifold Mercies bestowed upon us, believe it to be our Duty, publickly to assemble together, to offer to him our grateful Acknowledgments, and the Tribute of Divine Worship:———— We do therefore, unite ourselves together as Members of this Religious Society, called by some, the "Free Quakers:" a Society established upon the enlarged and benevolent Principles of the Gospel, and hope to profess true Christian Charity, even that Divine Love, which enlargeth the Heart towards all Men, and leadeth to hope and believe; that however divided the Church militant on Earth, may be, that yet the Church triumphant in Heaven is made up of all Nations, Kindreds, Tongues and People, who with the Harps of God in their Hands are praising him on Mount Zion.

We think it proper to add, as we have heretofore declared in an Address published, in the early Institution of this Society," that we have no Design to form Creeds "or Confessions of Faith, but humbly to confide in those "sacred Lessons of Wisdom and Benevolence which have "been left us by Christ and his Apostles contained in the "Holy Scriptures, and appealing to that Divine principle

"breathed"

- breathed by the Breath of God into the Hearts of all
- Men, to leave every Man to think and judge for himself,
- according to the Abilities received, and to answer for his
- Faith and Opinions to him who seeth the Secrets of all
- Hearts, the sole Judge and sovereign Lord of Conscience."

    Being now through divine Favour, in some measure established as a religious Society, we trust by an Adherence to those Catholic Principles, we shall be favoured with the Blessing of the Almighty, and therefore relying upon him for Protection, We do hereunto subscribe our own Names, and the Names of our Children, as Brethren and Sisters in Community, the seventeenth day of the Second Month (called February) in the Year of our Lord One Thousand Seven hundred and Eighty five. 1785.

Isaac Howell	Lydia Darragh
Peter Thomson	Sarah Wetherill Decd.
Thomas Renshaw	Elinor Karcher
Samuel Crispin	Ann Lewton
Nathaniel Browne	Ann Darah
Moses Bartram	Susanna Darragh
Saml. Wetherill Jr.	Isabella Renshaw
Jehu Eldredge	Sarah Paschall
John Piles	Elizabeth Parry
Edward Riffetts	Esther Parry
Benjamin Say	Susen Smallwood

THE PRECEDING PAGE AND THESE TWO PAGES ARE FROM THE REVISED MEMBERSHIP BOOK OF THE FREE QUAKERS, INSCRIBED AFTER REMOVAL TO THEIR NEW MEETING HOUSE. THE PREAMBLE IS IN THE FINE HANDWRITING OF ONE OF THEIR NUMBER, PETER THOMSON, WHO

Joseph Warner   Charity Warner
William Darragh   Mary Lawn
Rowd Parry   Elizabeth Thomson
Samuel Eldredge   Lidia Crispin
T. Matlack   Elizabeth Neave
Jonathan Scholfield   Elizabeth Neave Jnr.
Rebecah Scholfield   Hannah Carmalt
Jacob Lahn   Elizabeth Claypoole
William Thomson   Margaretta Rinfrinim
Samuel Crispin Senn   Sarah Wetherill Daughter of
William Milnor   Samuel Wetherill & Sarah his Wife
Elex Lewis   Mary Crisps ... pr Order
Wm. Matlack   Martha Wetherby pr Order
Samuel Wetherill Minr.   Thomas Lang — Margaret
Mord Wetherill   Wife of Thomas Lang, and
John Wetherill   Margaret & Agnes his
Rachy Forners   daughters.
William Smallwood   James Lang
John Claypoole   Mary Elton
Jacob Confer   Susannah Elton
George Kemble   John Elton
Thomas Elton   Thomas Elton
    Elizabeth Elton
    Anthony Elton

ACTED AS SCRIVENER FOR THE CONTINENTAL CONGRESS. HE IT WAS WHO
ENGROSSED THE DECLARATION OF INDEPENDENCE UPON PARCHMENT TO
BE SIGNED BY THE MEMBERS OF THE CONGRESS. ON THIS PAGE OF THE
BOOK ARE THE SIGNATURES OF JOHN AND ELIZABETH CLAYPOOLE

17

tinues as a charitable organization. Descendants of the founders and others who have joined it for its philanthropic work meet once a year at the old Meeting House to dispense the income from old properties owned by the Society to the city's poor.

The declining years of Elizabeth Claypoole were spent in the peace and happiness of visits at the homes of her married daughters. After her husband's death, she lived for a time with her second daughter, Susannah, wife of Abel Satterthwaite, a well-to-do Philadelphia hardware merchant, at his country home in Abington. This old stone house on the Jenkintown - Fox Chase road is still standing. It was her custom to go by stage out the old familiar Second Street Pike to Fox Chase, alight at the inn which is still a landmark in that village, and there wait for a member of her daughter's household to drive in for her. Betsy's brightness and charm and her keen interest in current events, even at this advanced age, were long remembered by those who knew her.

Seven presidents of the United States held office between the close of the Revolution and the end of her long and eventful life. Betsy Ross saw the country spread from a narrow strip along the Atlantic seaboard far beyond the Mississippi. She saw the thirteen stars of the flag she helped to create double in number as succeeding States came into the Union. These thirteen stars, embodying the motto "A Star for every State and a State for every Star," have now grown to forty-eight.

Though Mrs. Claypoole often related the story of the first flag to her daughters, neither she nor they realized the great historical significance it was to assume. To her the most important thing about it was the visit of the august Washington to her little home and shop. The act of designing and arranging the stars for a tentative flag was but an incidental feature.

Such matters of sentiment received but scant attention in the early and struggling days of the republic. Even the old State House, now known as Independence Hall, and the Liberty Bell were but indifferently regarded until near the middle of the nineteenth century. Moreover, the daughters and grandchildren of Betsy Ross Claypoole, growing up as strict members of the Society of Friends, talked but little of the flag episode because of its military aspects. The whole subject of Revolutionary disownments and subsequent reinstatements was seldom referred to by Quakers, even in the families of the disowned. Betsy's early life was hardly one to be mentioned with pride for two reasons. She was expelled from the faith and she was militaristic in her views.

As time wore on, however, and the Stars and Stripes increased in fame and influence, its origin became a subject of nation-wide interest. The facts spread far beyond the Quaker circle, and the Flag House in Arch Street is today a historic shrine visited annually by patriotic thousands.

The manner in which this little dwelling, which changed hands several times in the century following the Revolution, was preserved to the nation is a story in itself which need not be detailed here. To Charles H. Weisgerber, a young artist who came back from his studies in Paris in 1891, and interested himself in the house, most of the credit is due. His painting depicting the interview of General Washington with the young widow, Mrs. Ross, attracted wide attention. Soon afterward, he started the movement which resulted in the organization of the American Flag House and Betsy Ross Memorial Association and the acquisition of the Flag House through the purchase of membership certificates by the public at large. People of every State in the Union and our island possessions; of every creed and every walk of life, including tens of thousands of school children, subscribed their dimes to the cause.

*   *   *   *   *   *

Betsy Ross Claypoole died on the thirtieth of January, 1836, at the age of eighty-four years. The end came at the home of her daughter, Jane Claypoole Canby, in Philadelphia, at 63 Cherry Street—after weeks of gradual decline.   In those final days, she talked much of her troublous early life, of the flag, of war incidents, and of the widowhood thrice brought to her by the conflict. Perhaps on Sabbath mornings, as she lay in her daughter's home, close by the scenes of her girlhood, these memories were intensified in her mind, as, in the words of "Evangeline,"

Distant and soft on her ear fell the chimes from the belfry of Christ Church
While intermingled with these, across the meadows were wafted
Sounds of psalms, that were sung by the Swedes in their church at Wicaco.

*Soft as descending wings fell the calm of the hour on **her**
    spirit:*
*Something within her said, "At length thy trials are
    ended."*

With the simple rites of the Friends, she was
buried beside her husband in the graveyard of the
Free Quakers, Fifth Street below Locust. When
this ground was later taken by the city for building purposes, their bodies were removed to Mount
Moriah Cemetery beyond the Schuylkill, where a
plain granite monument erected by the Patriotic
Order Sons of America in 1923 marks their last rest-
ing place. A bronze plate, surrounded by a wreath
containing thirteen stars, bears the following:

TO HONOR THE MAKER
of the
FIRST AMERICAN FLAG
ELIZABETH GRISCOM
ROSS
ASHBOURN
CLAYPOOLE
1752 to 1836
BETSY ROSS

Appendix

SUMMARY OF HISTORICAL EVIDENCE RELATING TO THE LIFE OF BETSY ROSS

Her parentage, birth, dates of marriages, and births of her children. Claypoole family Bible, containing entries in her own handwriting and that of John Claypoole; *Genealogy of the Claypoole Family of Philadelphia*, by Rebecca Irwin Graff; *Genealogy of the Satterthwaite Family*, by Amos and Elizabeth Satterthwaite; Chart of Griscom Family of Philadelphia, completed by Ann Griscom in 1866, in possession of Historical Society of Pennsylvania.

Membership of Samuel Griscom, father of Betsy Ross, and Tobias Griscom, her grandfather, in Carpenters' Company. Old minute books and membership roll in Carpenters' Hall.

Record of Samuel Griscom's Arch Street residence. Survey for insurance policy granted by The Philadelphia Contributionship, the oldest fire insurance company in America, on new house built and occupied by him—dated August 2, 1764. To this house (one block west of the Flag House) the family moved when Betsy was twelve years old. Samuel Griscom's name is on a parchment scroll containing 1774 names of early members of the company, one of Philadelphia's prized relics of Colonial days.

Betsy Griscom's marriage to John Ross and disownment by the Quakers. Colonial records of the Society of Friends, minutes of Monthly Meetings of Northern District for year 1774. Also *Rossiana*, by Major Harmon P. Read.

Death and burial of John Ross. Records of Old Christ Church for year 1776.

Making of Stars and Stripes for Washington and two members of the Continental Congress, prior to Declaration of Independence in 1776. Statements of Betsy Ross as preserved in affidavits by niece (who later worked at flag-making with her), and others who knew her.

Evidence that Betsy Ross did make flags during Revolution. Minutes of State Navy Board, Pennsylvania Archives, dated May 29, 1777, ordering Treasurer to pay her for ship's colors. Volume I, Second Series, Pennsylvania Archives, states, referring to this: "The first colors made for the fleet that we have any record of were made by Elizabeth Ross of Philadelphia."

Evidence that these colors could not have been a State flag and very possibly were the new national emblem. "Pennsylvania Manual" (1929 issue, page 243), which asserts that Pennsylvania as a colony had no flag, so far as known, and that as a State it had none until 1799.

Official adoption of Stars and Stripes as the Flag of the United States. Journals of Congress, June 14, 1777.

Evidence that Flag may have been in use in meantime. Paintings by Charles Willson Peale and John Trumbull, who fought under Washington. Battle scenes show

Stars and Stripes used by Washington six months before Congress officially recognized it.

Marriage of Betsy Ross to Captain Joseph Ashburn. Revolutionary records of Old Swedes' Church, June 15, 1777.

Part taken by Claypooles in War, including John Claypoole's commission as Second Lieutenant. *Pennsylvania in the Revolution, 1775-1783,* Vol. I. Also *Genealogy of the Claypoole Family of Philadelphia.*

Sailing of Joseph Ashburn on his last voyage. Pennsylvania Archives, Vol. I, Fifth Series.

Sailing of John Claypoole on privateer *Luzerne.* John Claypoole's Journal.

Their capture by the British, their meeting in Old Mill Prison, and Ashburn's death. John Claypoole's Journal.

Hardships in "Old Mill." Diary of Charles Herbert and memoirs of Andrew Sherburne.

Marriage of Claypoole to Betsy Ross Ashburn. Claypoole family Bible. Also *Genealogy of the Claypoole Family.*

Their membership in "Fighting Quakers." Old records, Society of Free Quakers. Also *History of the Free Quakers,* by Charles Wetherill, descendant of the founder.

Record of residence of John and Betsy Claypoole. White's Philadelphia Directory, published in 1785, listing "John Claypoole, upholsterer, Arch street, between Second and Third streets."

Record of final residence of Betsy Ross's parents at time of their deaths in great Yellow Fever Epidemic. Clement Biddle's Philadelphia Directory of 1791, listing "Samuel Griscom, house carpenter, 54 Vine street."

Affidavits

The following affidavits are two of many statements, all of similar import, made by individuals who were closely associated with Betsy Ross (Elizabeth Claypoole) or knew her personally:

MRS. MARGARET BOGGS

A NIECE OF BETSY ROSS (DAUGHTER OF HER SISTER SARAH), WHO WAS FOR YEARS ASSOCIATED WITH HER IN THE FLAG-MAKING BUSINESS

I, Margaret Boggs, of the City of Philadelphia, widow, do hereby certify that I have heard my aunt, Elizabeth Claypoole, say many times that she made the first Star Spangled Banner that ever was made, with her own hands; that she made it on the order of General Washington and a committee of the Continental Congress, who together called personally upon her at her house on the north side of Arch street below Third street, Philadelphia, some time previously to the Declaration of Independence. That they brought with them a drawing roughly made, of the proposed flag; that she said it was wrong, and proposed alterations, which Washington and the committee approved; that one of these alterations was in regard to the number of points of the star; that she said it should be five-pointed, and showed them how to fold a piece of paper in the proper manner, and with one cut of the scissors, to make a five-pointed star; that General Washington sat at the table in her back parlor, where they were, and made a drawing of the flag, embodying her suggestions, and that she made the flag according to this drawing, and the committee carried it before Congress, by whom it was approved and adopted. That she then received orders to make flags for the government as fast as possible; and from that time, forward for upwards of 50 years, she made flags for the United States in Philadelphia, and largely for the other naval stations. I was for many years a member of her family and aided her in the business. I believe the facts stated in the foregoing article, entitled "The First American Flag, and Who Made It," which has now been read to me, are all strictly true.

WITNESS my hand at Germantown in the City of Philadelphia, this third day of June, A. D., 1870.

Margaret Boggs

(NOTE: The article, "The First American Flag, and Who Made It," referred to by Mrs. Boggs, was a manuscript written by William J. Canby, a grandson of Betsy Ross.)

SOPHIA B. HILDEBRANDT
A Granddaughter, Who Also Helped in the Flag-making in Its Later Years

I remember to have heard my grandmother, Elizabeth Claypoole, frequently narrate the circumstance of her having made the first Star-Spangled Banner; that it was a specimen flag made to the order of a Committee of Congress, acting in conjunction with General Washington, who called upon her personally at her store in Arch Street, below Third Street, Philadelphia, shortly before the Declaration of Independence; that she said that General Washington made a redrawing of the design with his own hands after some suggestions made by her; and that this specimen flag and report were approved and adopted by Congress; and she received an unlimited order from the Committee to make flags for the government; and to my knowledge she continued to manufacture government flags for about fifty years, when my mother succeeded her in the business, in which I assisted. I believe the facts stated in the foregoing article, entitled, "The First American Flag, and Who Made It," are all strictly true.

Witness my hand at Philadelphia, the twenty-seventh day of May, A.D., 1870.

S. B. Hildebrandt

Affirmed and subscribed before
Charles H. Evans, Notary Public.

(NOTE: History shows that it was not until a year after the committee's interview with Betsy Ross that Congress actually approved the flag, though circumstances point to its use in the meantime. It is believed that Robert Morris, a member of the committee, personally defrayed the cost of many of the flags ordered of Mrs. Ross. He often helped General Washington in emergencies of this character from his ample means when Congress was short of funds, sometimes coming to the rescue when payments of soldiers were in arrears. As the head of the Marine Committee during a great part of the war, the flag question was an important one to him.

* * * * * * *

Mrs. Sophia Hildebrandt, named above, was a daughter of Mrs. Clarissa S. Wilson, Betsy Ross's oldest daughter, who was active in the flag-making and carried it on following her mother's death. The originals of the above affidavits and other statements are now in the possession of Dr. Lloyd Balderston, a great-grandson of Betsy Ross.)

Index